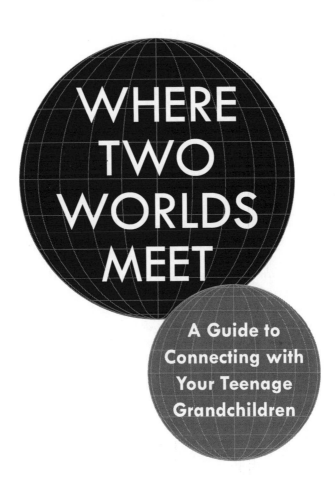

WHERE TWO WORLDS MEET

A Guide to Connecting with Your Teenage Grandchildren

JERRY WITKOVSKY & DEANNA SHOSS

North Carolina

Originally edited by Beth Lieberman and Vivien Orbach-Smith

Published in the United States by WriteLife Publishing
(an imprint of Boutique of Quality Books Publishing Company, Inc.)
www.writelife.com

978-1-60808-272-8 (p)
978-1-60808-273-5 (e)

Library of Congress Control Number: 2022937330

Book Design by Robin Krauss, www.bookformatters.com
Cover Design by Rebecca Lown, www.rebeccalowndesign.com
First editor: Andrea Vande Vorde
Second editor: Allison Itterly

PRAISE FOR
WHERE TWO WORLDS MEET

"This wonderful book, *Where Two Worlds Meet: A Guide to Connecting with Your Teenage Grandchildren*, is full of real world tools to help the two generations find common ground. From letters, to organized meetings, to determining a family legacy, these methods are sure to bring eager grandparents and busy older grandchildren together around important common goals. I recommend it to all grandparents!"

– Elizabeth LaBan, author of *Beside Herself*;
Not Perfect; *The Restaurant Critic's Wife*;
The Tragedy Paper; *The Grandparents Handbook*;
and co-author of *Pretty Little World*

"In *Where Two Worlds Meet*, Witkovsky and Shoss have created a must-have manual for grandparents seeking intentional, impactful connections with grandchildren progressing from preteen into adulthood—that tough period when kids naturally pull away. Sage advice, actionable items, journaling prompts, and stories from grandparents and grandchildren reflecting on their bond provide a practical guide for all grandparents, whether long-distance, local, or sharing a multigenerational household.

– Lisa Carpenter, founder of GrandmasBriefs.com and author of *"The First-Time Grandmother's Journal*

"Where Two Worlds Meet: A Guide to Connecting with Your Grandchildren" is a book built on passion, real-life experience, hope, and the power of love. Witkovsky and his associate Shoss, share Witkovsky's life-long commitment to strengthening and celebrating the bonds that make families grow while maximizing the potential and individuality of each of the family members."

– Bruce Mondschain, Catalyst Associates

"Where Two Worlds Meet is a Must-Have Book! The authors provide such creative and innovative ways to connect with grandchildren and as a grandparent and former school principal I highly recommend this book."

– Debbie Saviano, Social Media Strategist, and Speaker

"If you are looking for valuable patterns for enhancing relationships between grandparents and teenage grandchildren—and for experiences, ideas, and stories galore, particularly about creating three-generational values and preserving cultural values, this book should be on your list."

– Linda and Richard Eyre, New York Times #1 Bestselling Authors whose most recent books are *Grandmothering* and *Being a Proactive Grandfather*

I dedicate this book to the memory of my wife,
Margaret, my partner for fifty-two years;
To my daughter, Ellen, and her husband, Don;
my son, Michael, and his wife, Julie;
and to the people who are my world and whose world
I never want to leave:
my grandchildren and their growing families—
Aidan, Merete, Benny and his wife, Corina;
Kathryn and her husband, Lance;
Ethan and his wife, Erin: parents of my
great-grandchildren, Aldo and Sage Margaret;
Jessica and her husband, Travis.

—Jerry Witkovsky

Banana cake and noodle kugel, fierce independence, and an entrepreneurial spirit are some of the gifts from my long and wonderful relationships with all four of my grandparents: Lydia, Lou, Ethel, and James. This book is dedicated to them and to my parents, Sammy and Bill, and to Vovó Antonia for being such phenomenal and involved grandparents.

I'm grateful for my husband, Eugênio; our son, Lucca (the teenager!); and my sisters Brenda and Cara, for her support as this book evolved. And this book is dedicated to Jerry Witkovsky, who inspires me every day with his creativity, commitment, and passion for grandparenting. He teaches us that, like a rocket, life is an upward trajectory. You never stop learning, creating, and contributing.

—Deanna Shoss

If you look deeply into the palm of your hand, you will see your parents and all generations of your ancestors.
All of them are alive in this moment.
Each is present in your body.
You are the continuation of each of these people.

—Thich Nhat Hanh

CONTENTS

INTRODUCTION

When grandchildren are young, a sweet treat, a new toy, or a visit to the museum is enough to inspire their unconditional adoration. Then your grandchildren grow up. Suddenly they are teenagers and it's not so easy.

Where Two Worlds Meet starts with the teenage years, a time when your grandchildren are discovering who they want to be as independent beings in the world. This book is about how to understand what life looks like through your grandchild's eyes, and how to invite your grandchildren to experience what life is like for you.

Sure, you live on the same planet, perhaps the same country, or even the same house, but you sense a distance growing between you and your grandchildren. There are so many reasons for this. It is developmentally on-target for teens to pull away from those they love, as their brains undergo massive change starting around age twelve. While that may be a solid, science-based explanation, it sure doesn't make it any easier as your teenage grandchildren turn away from you and toward their peers for trusted answers to everything. They are more involved in school activities, and academics are more demanding. You, too, may also be adapting to a new stage of life. As you near retirement and plan for what's next, you have a wonderful opportunity to travel and visit family, pursue hobbies, or take classes. You are also adjusting to all the body and energy changes that come with aging.

And perhaps you find yourself in a world that has changed so much, and not always for the better. This can be hard to comprehend.

You and your grandchild are from different generations, each with its own fashion and music, pop stars, technology, and world-framing events. And there is no doubt about it: the generation into which a person is born has a profound impact on that individual's view of the world. Indeed, even teenage behavior is defined by its generation. Think of the teens who went off to World War II, those who attended Woodstock, or a how a teen today can start a global movement with their ideas and access to the internet.

Our teenage grandchildren need us now more than ever. In 2021, the Surgeon General declared kids in crises—particularly with COVID and its variants, depression and suicide among teens is the highest it has ever been. Grandparents are uniquely prepared to help, support, and relate to their teenage grandchildren. We've lived through the Holocaust, the Great Depression, the polio epidemic, Vietnam and the draft—we've got the life experience of survivors. As grandparents, we must do everything we can to be there for our grandchildren. We would do that no matter what. This book gives you the how.

Where Two Worlds Meet explores the grandparent-grandchild relationship through an intergenerational lens. It provides real tactics you can use to create a culture in your family where sharing is a two-way street, and that will bring you and your grandchild, and your whole family, closer together. That's super critical in today's environment where the future is so uncertain.

I'm delighted to bring you on this amazing journey with me. I'm your narrator, Jerry Witkovsky. Like you, I am a grandparent wildly in love with my grandchildren, who—like yours—are the most amazing, brilliant, attractive, and accomplished grandchildren in all the world. My late wife, Margaret, and I were blessed with six of them: three girls and three boys born between 1983 and 2002, and two great-grandchildren born in 2017 and 2020.

For the last sixty years, grandparenting has been the focus of my life and work. From the moment I earned my Master of Social Work (MSW) in 1952, I focused on youth programming, but always as it connected back to the whole family. As a residential camp director in Wisconsin, I introduced the first grandparents weekend in 1970, inviting grandparents to see firsthand the exuberance of their grandchildren immersed in the camp environment.

Many were inspired to join in, taking a turn on the zip line or the climbing wall. That sure was a delightful surprise for grandparents and grandchildren! As General Director of the Jewish Community Center (JCC) of Chicago, I transformed the mission of the organization to focus on the dynamics of the entire family, from early childhood through older adults. Along the way I have researched and lectured about grandparenting issues, developed community and school-based programs that allow intergenerational bonds to flourish, and facilitated support groups for grandparents.

Even though these grandparents were a diverse group, their concerns were startlingly similar. Things like:

- How do I stay connected to grandchildren, especially as they grow up and I age?

- How can I play an active role in nurturing my grandchildren when I've had a less-than-ideal relationship with one, or both, of their parents?

- With all the stresses and distractions of modern life, how can our family unit be truly supportive of each other, enrich each other's lives, and create lasting memories?

- What is my personal legacy to this family? And what can I do to make an impact, or to impart something of value while I'm still around?

Where Two Worlds Meet shifts the power from "How do I make it happen?" to "How do we build it together?"

My creative partner and coauthor, Deanna Shoss, calls me a "grandparenting activist." I speak across the country, set up programs for grandparents at area schools, and I'm featured on the radio, TV, and in the news. I'm particularly proud of the *Grandparents! Write Your Stories* program, created with the JCC and YMCA of Chicago, with hundreds of grandparents from three continents signing up to receive writing prompts for stories to share with their grandchildren. In this book, you'll hear my stories as well as those of grandparents I've encountered along the way.

While you might not hear directly from Deanna in the pages of this book, you'll see her partnership throughout. She is not yet a grandma, but she does know about entering the worlds of other people. Deanna speaks four languages and relishes life in her Jewish-Brazilian interfaith, intercultural family. She also adds her perspective as the adult child and the parent of a teenager, applying the tools in this book to her own family. Deanna is a long-time marketer and intercultural writer, trainer, and researcher. She has helped me take the tenets of cultural competence—self-awareness, empathy, flexibility, curiosity, and tolerance for ambiguity—and apply them to deepening the grandparent-grandchild connection. Grandparenting is all about the love. Our goal by using some of the ideas from interculturalism and intergenerational exchange is to help you be the most powerful and engaged grandparent you can be.

Thanks to increased longevity, many of us may have *forty or more years* to participate in the lives of our grandchildren! And that's not the only good news. Living near each other (or having the means to undertake regular visits) is no longer essential to maintaining close family ties thanks to burgeoning communications technologies and easy-access social networks that are being embraced by older adults in record numbers. This translates into a wealth of opportunities for us to have a profound and enduring mutual connection with our grandchildren.

Each chapter of this book focuses on an action you can take to bring your family together across the generations. You can read them in order or start with the chapter you want to explore first. There are fun activities to gain perspective on each other's generation. You'll learn how to exchange stories with your grandchildren to forge bonds around common life milestones, regardless of age. You'll also learn how to give voice to your values and to add meaning to your time together with your grandchildren. Chapter 9 has specific initiatives you can do now to understand your legacy and know how you inspire your grandchildren. And you'll get a chance to make amends, if needed, with the generation in between: your grandchildren's parents (your adult children). How can you navigate your interdependence, practice forgiveness, and heal old wounds? That's all part of the process of seeing things from another person's perspective. That's the power of entering each other's world.

These concepts are applicable to all kinds of families. You bring the values. You provide the ideas, talents, and experiences. What this book teaches are skills to allow you to bring your whole self to the relationship, how to embrace your grandchild and let them see you— complete with your struggles and triumphs and as a full person, not only in your relationship to them. Experience the world as they see it and don't be afraid to let them into your world.

The benefits of consciously and deliberately entering each other's world are powerful for all involved:

- Grandparents are able to impart wisdom without lording over the rest of the family. They show themselves to be flexible thinkers who are open to new ideas.

- Adult children may see a different side of their parents by hearing new stories shared with grandchildren. And adult parents get support during these more challenging teenage years.

- Teenage grandchildren who are made to feel that their perspective and experiences matter, that they are truly heard, are less likely to tune out the voices of others. They develop pride and confidence in their own ideas and accomplishments and aren't so quick to view their elders as prehistoric purveyors of obsolete notions.

Typically, sharing families will debate vigorously about *ideas.* Disagreements inevitably happen at some point. Whether they are about current events, personal beliefs, or where to go for dinner, they just aren't automatically as aggressively personal when every member actively tries to enter the other's world and at least tries to understand their perspective even if they don't agree. When nobody's on the attack, nobody's on the defensive. Even as everyone's priorities, interests, and experiences change with age, the approach of sharing your world with your family generates a mutual trust that will grow along with you.

Journaling Expeditions

At the end of each chapter, you'll find Journaling Expeditions. These are questions and prompts to inspire you to adapt what you learned from each chapter to your own family and relationship with your grandchildren.

I encourage you to get a notebook or create a document on your computer to accompany your reading of this book. Write down your answers and commit to acting.

I also urge you to share your questions and answers with your adult children and grandchildren along the way to let them know of your commitment and desire to connect more deeply with them.

Letters from Grandchildren, Stories from Grandparents

Don't take only my word for it—this book is peppered with amazing letters from grandchildren representing a diversity of ages and backgrounds who submitted their stirring personal memories about a grandparent's impact on their lives.

A number of the contributors are either professional or aspiring writers, but many are not. Some of their reflections are charming, some are immensely uplifting, and all are full of love and admiration. Interestingly, among our respondents, more than one is a grandchild of Holocaust survivors. Their deeply poignant reflections illustrate that even families marked by epic trauma and loss have the capacity to regenerate and become wellsprings for inspiration and positive living.

You'll also see stories from other grandparents I know who share their challenges as grandparents and their successes with implementing the ideas in this book.

I hope this chorus of voices, together with my own, will send forth the message that grandparents really matter, and that a grandparent's light—whether it shines

CHAPTER 1

Bring Your Whole Self to the Relationship

Grandparents can have a transformative effect on their family when they unleash their creativity, share their unique talents, and give voice to the things they are passionate about. I don't mean creativity in terms of specific arts like painting or poetry, although these are great to share. Creativity is about the way in which you bring your whole self to the relationship with your grandchildren, including all your assets and a willingness to be vulnerable.

We don't always know what will stick with our grandchildren, the things they will learn from us, and what they will remember most. Unless you ask. Throughout this book, I invited grandchildren, including my own, to contribute letters about what they had learned from a grandparent. In true contrarian teenager fashion, my grandson Benny, age seventeen at the time he wrote this, spent much of the letter explaining to me why I was wrong.

Respect for Conviction Even
in Disagreement

I am confused—but then again, so are you. I'm not sure if this letter is supposed to be about specific things—ideas, skills, bits of wisdom—that I have learned from you. Or if it is supposed to be about the way I watch you interact with the world and how I see those same traits in myself. And I don't think you know what you want the letter to be about either.

That's why I think what really interests you is the way of "being" that you have passed on. But then why is that something that should be written and published? I have told you before, so I think you know. And how does it serve as a teaching tool?

You cannot change or craft your way of being to teach me. As I believe I have told you, "You don't get to choose what I watch and learn from you; it happens no matter what." So, the family is a tool for teaching personality, intentionally and unintentionally, without a letter or a meeting or a plan.

Then I realize that I said this to you some

five or six years ago. You have always been concerned with how the grandparent ensures that their essence is passed on either through a living legacy, teachable moments, or a family learning community.

It is that commitment to an idea that I have learned from you. I have watched you redefine your quest as you have been turned down, encouraged, and questioned. I have seen you take some criticism and ignore others. And I have learned how to explore an idea that you know has some inherent truth but that you are ceaselessly morphing and searching for the best way to define, understand, and present.

I don't know what my idea will be yet, but I hope I own it with the same conviction.

Love,
Benny (written at 17)

For me, bringing my whole self to the relationship meant leading with my business background, which was integral to my identity, and which I recognized as a strength that would help me connect with my family. That's who I am and what I know. For other grandparents, that might be your experience as a teacher, artist, doctor, or farmer. Embrace the power of who you are and use it to connect with your grandchildren.

Benny's letter captures one aspect that was important to me in my professional leadership roles: the power of setting an example and committing to action. Benny first challenged me about this idea when he was twelve. I will take that as a compliment to my consistent commitment to expressing my vision for my family. Benny is now finishing his doctoral thesis in sociology. He definitely has found his idea.

The Day Your First Grandchild Is Born

From the moment your first grandchild is born, you have the opportunity to begin building the memories your grandchildren will cherish forever. Everything you need is already within you. Bringing your whole self to the relationship is the key to igniting this magical connection.

My first grandchild was born in 1983. When we got to the hospital, my wife went in to be with our daughter. My son-in-law said to me, "Come on, I'll take you to meet your granddaughter." We walked down the hall to the nursery, and he pointed and said, "There's Jessica."

I tapped on the window and said, "Jessica. It's me. Grandpa." Nothing. So I tapped on the window again. Still nothing. I was going to walk away and then thought,

One more time. I tapped on the window. "It's Grandpa." Out came her arm from the cover. I imagined a great big smile, her moving hand certainly must be an intentional wave. Then she put her arm back in and fell asleep.

That's when I got hooked. I experienced that feeling of walking on air the moment I laid eyes on each of my grandchildren, starting that day with Jessica.

Love and Caring Prevails

Grandparenting a teenager can take a leap of faith. It's going to be hard, especially when it feels like they are emotionally blocking you or simply don't have time to spend with you anymore. Now is the time to double down on your giving of unconditional love and caring. You know in your heart that your grandchildren love you, even as they are rolling their eyes or saying hurtful things now that they are teenagers. Remind yourself that it's not personal. You know this because of your great history together. Remember the struggle of parenting your children when they were teens, or even your own behavior from when you were a teenager. (What would *your* parents say?) And remember the first time you fell in love with each of your grandchildren. You can almost conjure their baby smell, the feeling of them all swaddled in a blanket in your arms.

My Grandparenting Foundation

My grandparenting years started when I was still in the prime of my career as the general director of the JCCs of Chicago. Even after I had retired, I was still quite active, and remain so, as a consultant and a community volunteer. Given my many years in the field, I had long been cognizant of the important role that grandparents and extended families play in a child's life and development.

So, you might assume that my determination to be the very best grandfather I could be would have kicked in immediately. But that's not quite how it happened.

Like many of you today, I was very busy. Then there was a matter of distance. My son, Michael, and his family live in Madison, Wisconsin, a three-hour drive from my home in Chicago at the time. My daughter, Ellen, started raising her family in a neighboring Chicago suburb. She, her husband, and their two daughters relocated to Los Angeles when their daughters were eighteen and fourteen.

And there was another kind of distance too. Oh, we all got along quite well when we got together several times a year for Thanksgiving, Passover, and such, but—like in many families—along with the obvious love and affection, there were areas of wariness and contention that probably had been smoldering quietly since Michael and Ellen were teenagers.

I wasn't much different of a grandfather, I suppose, than I was a father. Which meant that I was very caring. And, did I mention, very busy?

It's been a grandparenting journey of almost four decades. But as far as being a planful grandparent, I'll begin on a beautiful fall day in 1992 when Margaret and I learned that Benny, who is our fourth grandchild, then just two years old, had suddenly taken ill and needed to be hospitalized. We immediately jumped into our car and drove to Madison to see how we could support our son's young family.

During those difficult days and nights in the pediatric ICU, I had a feeling that the four of us—Margaret and I, and Benny's frightened parents—were suspended together in another dimension. Stripped of our daily preoccupations and petty disagreements, we were remarkably in sync, bound by a common purpose. We needed to operate together as an effective team to do everything we could for Benny and his big brother, eight-year-old Ethan.

I have to say, we were quite the team. By truly listening to each other, focusing on our joint mission, and working to our individual strengths, we mapped out a workable plan: who would pick up Ethan at school, who would stay with Benny, who would get the groceries, who would field the nonstop phone calls, and so on. Without fear, embarrassment, or recrimination, we were able to

be honest with each other, too, about who might need a
break and who might need a hug, who yearned for an
encouraging word or a place to pray, and who wanted
to be left alone.

Throughout Benny's illness and subsequent recuper-
ation, as the circumstances changed, so did our plan.

After the ordeal had passed, I was indescribably
relieved that Benny was doing so well and proud of how
each of us had managed to step up to the plate. Yet, one
thing nagged at me. I wondered: Why does it always
take events like this to make people genuinely attuned
to each other's needs and to be fully present for one
another? Why should it take near tragedy to remind us
how much we value and rely on each other? Of course,
these are the questions that most of us ask ourselves at
critical life junctures. All too often, however, after that
crisis passes, so does our resolve.

And sure enough, as Benny blessedly returned to full
health, our busy family returned to business as usual.
This left me with more questions. Outside of a crisis,
when it comes to the enormously complex dance of
human relationships, how can we possibly know what's
in another person's heart and what their true hierarchy
of goals is? How can we possibly know their convictions,
their struggles, or their deepest yearnings? We can't
know unless we actively seek to find out. That process
of finding out is a basic tenet of my training as a social

worker. It starts with self-awareness and the practice of looking deeply into the soul of who you are to better serve others. It dawned on me that this seasoned social worker needed to look deep into the soul of his *own* family unit and apply to his own life what he knew to be effective models to foster genuine communication, connection, and growth.

To bring your whole self to the relationship means you are aware of all that you offer and that you are willing to embrace discomfort by exposing your vulnerability in sharing everything with your grandchildren and adult children. That needs to be your guiding framework as a grandparent.

Start Where You Are with What You Know

Bringing my whole self to the forefront with my grand-children wasn't easy at first. It had been a long time since I had been around babies and toddlers. Because I was the director of a children's camp for ages eight through sixteen, I felt like I was supposed to know all of the right things to do when it came to children of all ages. Yet I was afraid to say the wrong thing and be rejected by my grandchildren. As a social worker, I was more concerned about their development and emotional state, asking them questions about how they felt, rather than what their favorite ice cream flavor was. Engaging with youngsters seemed to come so naturally to my wife, Margaret. She was a tirelessly creative and fun grandmother, always ready to pull out her craft materials or to play a spirited game of Scrabble. Those were her things and how she interacted with our grandchildren, but I wanted to find my own identity in how I connected with my grandchildren.

I fell back on what I knew best: my business and management experience. Managers know how to identify and fill a skill gap. My learning deficit at the time was how to relate to toddlers. Good managers start with research, and they are not afraid to ask questions and admit what they don't know. I asked my adult children, "What do my grandchildren like to do for fun? What are their favorite snacks, books, toys, and places to go?" I bought all of their favorites and made a "Grandpa's Fun Box" that was theirs to explore whenever they came over.

As a supervisor, I had always emphasized the importance of developing a customized plan of action to solve a problem. In fact, I had a very specific four-step process that I used when counseling families in duress. Time and again, I had witnessed how this process had been a life preserver that helped drowning families survive despite major obstacles. I wondered if I could apply the same process to bringing my full self to my relationship with my grandchildren. Here's what that looked like, following the process I used in my work.

Step 1: Identify a group's needs and objectives by asking the right questions of all its members and really listen to their individual answers. Here is where I may have been overthinking it. The objective with grandchildren at that stage of their life was to keep them safe and have fun. Perhaps I needed to relax a little!

Step 2: Ensure that every individual's unique strengths and opportunities for growth are taken into account. This was where Margaret really shined with her formal training as an artist. This was also where I benefitted from leaning into what I knew rather than focusing on what I didn't know.

Step 3: Codify any issues by writing things down so it's not left to memory or to chance, and so that one day the parties are able to look back on what was written and get a true picture of how far they've come.

For me, this meant journaling to celebrate successes and explore my fears. Never one to stay stuck, as soon as I recognized a concern, I immediately wrote questions to solve it. What size ball is right for them to play with at this stage? What should we do when we run out of space on the refrigerator for their artwork? How can we prepare the room for painting? Journaling was my way of preparing to be fully present when I was with my grandchildren. I needed to write and plan and prepare. I didn't need to share that part with them. But I did need to acknowledge that bringing my full self to the relationship with my grandchildren took practice and process.

Step 4: Take immense care that all interactions are rooted in courtesy, compassion, and respect. This practice was easy to transfer to home and family. I would also add love and caring.

I applied this four-step process to help myself when my grandchildren were young and when Margaret and I were first learning to be the best grandparents that we could be. As my grandchildren age, I have used this process over and over to learn and develop as a grandparent. I now engage them and their parents as partners in this process, allowing all of us to *thrive*.

A thriving, powerful family is about more than just me and my relationship with my growing grandchildren. It is about multidirectional relationships between grandchildren, parents, and grandparents, and how all of us can connect more deeply across the generations. Every member of the family has something to share.

The Door to Their World Is Different
for Each Grandchild

To fully enter your grandchild's world, you first must find a door. That's why it is so important to discover a mutually enjoyable entry point for connecting with each grandchild. I would discuss stocks with Benny, or play catch with Jessica, or stroll through the botanic garden with Kathryn, or watch documentaries with Ethan. These are all doorways into my world. Each grandchild embraces a different one. Once there, add depth. Benny wanted to talk more about how I chose which stocks to invest in, and he asked that I not buy stocks in companies that manufactured guns or profited from war. With Kathryn, we would pause to sit on a bench and listen to the bird sounds and try to identify them. Looking at the beauty and diversity of the plants led to a conversation about whether they were created by God or humans. As Jessica and I tossed tennis balls, I shared that I had been on the tennis team in high school and lost. "What was that like, Grandpa?" she asked, inviting a story.

If this sounds amazing and bucolic, it was. It is! Except for the times when it isn't.

It's Not You, It's Them!
Typical Behavior for the Teenage Years

With teenage grandchildren, sometimes it's hard just to settle on a time to get together with so much homework and extracurricular activities. Their storytelling stops too and is replaced by one- or two-word responses. You didn't see it coming. You might have been thinking, *Those poor other grandparents whose grandchildren won't talk to them.* Then it was your preteen or teenage grandchild who clammed up. It's not you! Remember, it is developmentally typical for adolescents to question adults and to want to spend more time with their peers. And that seems to start happening around the magical age of twelve.

We often talk of raging hormones at this stage as puberty hits. Physiologically, our grandchildren's brains are changing too. Their limbic system, which controls emotion, is fully online and functional. Their frontal lobe, however, which governs decision making, won't be fully developed for another thirteen years!

A few years ago, I ran a pilot program for the Grandparent-Grandchild Connection School Program at the Sager Solomon Schechter Day School in Deerfield, Illinois. As part of the presentation to grandparents on how to enter their grandchild's world at school, I asked the school's social worker, Rachael Gray-Raff, MA, MSW, to tell grandparents some of the changes they might see in their grandchildren as they entered middle school. Here are a few:

1. Their trusted go-to source for "the truth" has shifted from family to friends, which means they are beginning to challenge adult explanations.

2. They are more likely to engage in risky behavior and are more susceptible to peer pressure to fit in.

3. They might be moody and self-absorbed.

4. They are sensitive about their changing bodies and more concerned with personal appearance.

These are all behaviors that are developmentally expected at this age. Not all teenagers will exhibit them, and certainly not all the time. My colleague Norma, who is a grandparent and a social worker, recalled a time when her grandchild shouted "I hate you!" at her. Her response? "Aw, sweetie. You are being developmentally normative!" It dissipated the power of the moment because Norma didn't take it personally. Now that her grandchild is older, they even laugh together, remembering this moment. To be clear, however, it doesn't mean you can't have boundaries. You can say, "Please don't speak to me that way," if they are disrespectful. Share how it impacts you. You could say something like, "It hurts my feelings when you speak to me that way." Unconditional love for your grandchild is never about being a doormat.

Why You Have to Stay the Course

We hope that our grandchildren will be resilient when faced with the challenges of adolescent life. What greatly fosters resilience is a support system—the proverbial village—that makes children and adolescents feel secure, heard, and loved. I can't think of anything we can do for our grandchildren that is more valuable than to be leaders of that village.

Studies affirm that "secure attachment"—as in, you as a constant emotional presence with your steadfast unconditional love in your grandchildren's lives—"is associated with less engagement in high-risk behaviors, fewer mental health problems, and enhanced social skills and coping strategies."[1]

While they may not admit it, your grandchildren don't understand their own changed behavior now that they are teenagers. They need you now more than ever, with so many changes going on that are out of their control. You have to trust that they love you, and you have to trust yourself. That's what I mean by bringing

---

1 Marlene M. Moretti and Maya Peled, "Adolescent-Parent Attachment: Bonds that Support Healthy Development," *Pediatrics Child Health* 9, no. 8 (2004): 551–555, doi: 10.1093/pch/9.8.551.

your full self to the relationship, knowing you already have everything you need within you—your heart, your love, your talents, your creativity, your passion, and your commitment. Now is the time to dig deeper for patience, perseverance, and understanding.

Letters from Grandchildren: What I Learned from My Grandparent

If your grandchildren ever ask you what you want for your birthday or holidays, here's any easy idea that won't cost them anything and will be priceless to you: a letter that lets you know what they've learned from you and how you've influenced their lives. That's how you know the power of your love and your enduring role in the family.

Here are some samples of those letters. The first letter is written by my grandson Ethan, who shares some things he has learned, followed by cherished stories from other people's grandchildren. Note that in the second letter, Barbara was eighty when she wrote this letter about her grandmother. It goes to show you that a grandparent's imprint is forever.

From Faith to Tarot Cards

Dear Grandma Margaret,

I am in rabbinical school now, and I am working on ways of bringing an old religion to people through new technologies (and some old technologies too). My dad told me once that when I was born, you predicted this is what I would do with my life. Nice job. Actually, I think I learned a lot about faith from you. The predictions and star-chart stuff, not to mention tarot cards and previous lives, were perhaps all about your belief in the unseen and that there are forces at work in our universe that are beyond our mien but that we can tap into briefly and rudimentarily if we go about it in the right way.

In fact, Grandma, as I write this, I realize that I completely share your belief in the power and magic of the world around us, and that I would not be who I am today without it or without you. You taught me it is okay to have faith, and that belief and love of these things is not silly and doesn't make you silly. On that same note, you also taught me to enjoy the little things other people miss, and that there is cool stuff to be found in even little things like puzzles and wearing purple. Really, though, it was the big things that will stay with me and are the most influential in my life. Your sense of play, passion for life, discipline, and faith in a magical universe have all been transmitted to me through a combination of teaching and DNA. These things have been a part of making me who I am today, for better and for worse, and they will continue to guide me as I go forward. Thank you, Grandma, for all of the things you gave me, and for being a ready teacher and playmate.

Ethan (written at 26)

Summers on Grandma's Farm

My Grandma Nettie was an old-fashioned Midwestern farm wife. She and Grandpa had nine children whom they raised on a rented farm in central Illinois. I was her first grandchild, and I always felt I was her favorite, though many others came after me.

From the time I was a young child in the 1940s, I started spending summers with my grandparents. They had electricity but no running water and few other modern conveniences.

Grandma baked bread every other day and always made a miniature muffin-sized loaf just for me. She let me help her knead the bread and sometimes help her with the pies she baked for Sundays.

On Saturdays, we went into town to do the weekly grocery shopping at the local Red & White store. Occasionally, the store had cattle feed, which came in brightly patterned calico sacks; she would let me pick out the ones I liked best, and then used the material to make me a dress and matching bonnet.

She taught me so many things: skills like cooking and baking, gardening, and canning. Some of the skills didn't end up being that important in my life—like how to sneak an egg from under a sitting hen who was guarding her nest. But most of all, she instilled in me patience, kindness, and faith.

I owe her so much.

Barbara H. (80)
Naples, Florida

Planting the Marigolds

It was Grandpa McLaughlin who taught me life's grand lessons, in small increments—about work, responsibility, community, and play.

Grandpa sold insurance. Whenever I—and later, my brothers—would visit, he'd let us play with the typewriter, rubber stamps, and spinning desk chair in his home office. After going door to door to collect very small premiums from his clients, he would sit at the dining room table and sort the bills. He taught me to put them in order of value, to line them up (all facing the same way), to count them twice and then to fill out the deposit slips. Then we'd go to the bank, where he'd introduce me to all the tellers.

Best of all was when he taught me to garden. He let me dig up the dirt to loosen it and then use my fingers to create two rows and spread the marigold seeds as if I were sprinkling gold dust. *Cover it up, pat it down, and check on it every time you come to visit.* Those were my marigolds.

Today I am a grandmother of four, ages six to ten. They enjoy when we do art projects with my "grown-up" paints, tools, and techniques. They also like teaching me their latest Wii games, and how to do new things, like play games, on my iPad and phone.

Grandparenting is marigold seeds, kites, and zoos; it is pictures, school events, and gymnastics performances. But really, it is so much more than that. Hopefully, I will leave my grandchildren the gift of feeling loved and confident, and of caring about the world beyond themselves. And the gift of good memories, as I have, fifty years hence.

Denise M. (62)
New Canaan, Connecticut

Who Is Your Hero and Why?

I found the following essay in August 2003 while cleaning out my grandmother's apartment in Florida after she passed away at the age of ninety-three. I had attached a note saying: "Dear Grandma, I wrote this for my camp application in response to the question: 'Who is your hero and why?' I thought you might like a copy. I love you very, very much. Love, Alysa." The note was written in 1992 when I was twenty years old.

"Enjoy life. It is as easy as a positive attitude." Ask my grandmother for advice and she would tell you just that. Many years of life experience and my grandmother's eyes reflect that youth is a way of thinking—a mentality, not a measure of years. My grandmother is my inspiration, and that is why she is also my hero. Have you heard of the phrase, "Smile and the world smiles with you"? Well, the world smiles with my grandmother. Watching her in action, I have learned invaluable lessons to live by that I will carry on with me and teach my grandchildren someday.

My grandma always reminds me, "It is just as easy to be nice as it is to be mean." She taught me not to pass judgment on someone else because there is usually more going on inside than meets the eye. My grandma is a firm believer in the compliment. Like smiles, they go a long way and are not just free—they are priceless. Feeling good about oneself is the inner glow each one of us needs to survive. Compliments are easy to give, and their impact is without bounds. My grandma has definitely caught on to a good thing. I think I have too.

I still miss her every day as I try to live by her wisdom and by the love she left me as her lasting legacy.

Rabbi Alysa Mendelson-Graf (41)
Westport, Connecticut

Your Turn: Journaling Expeditions

Chapter 1 discusses having empathy for what it is like to be a teenager today, as well as tips on how to bring your full self to your relationship with your grandchildren. The following questions will help you brainstorm on how to apply these concepts to your life and your relationships.

1. Write down three to five things you remember about yourself when you were a teenager. What was important to you?

2. What do you remember about raising your adult children as they became teenagers and young adults?

3. What are three to five things you would like to do to deepen your relationship with your grandchil-

dren? Write them down and refer back to them as you work your way through this book.

4. What are the skills, talents, and hobbies you want to teach and share with your grandchildren?

CHAPTER 2

Bridge the Generations

Sixty-plus years ago, life as a twelve-year-old was vastly different than that of our budding teenage grandchildren today. Rosie, the robotic housekeeper on *The Jetsons*, is now a reality. We've gone from dreaming of the first space launch to commercial space travel. Computers, at one time the size of your house, can now fit into the palm of your hand. You and your grandchildren are from different generations. With our differences in musical tastes, technology, formative events, pop culture, and fashion, one could even say we are from different worlds. In the "olden days," we might sit tight in our position as "elder" of the family and expect that our grandchildren would come to us. Imagine the magic, however, if we open ourselves to new experiences and consciously try to understand our grandchildren's world and invite them to enter ours. That's the sweet spot where two worlds meet.

The power of bridging the generations and entering each other's world is palpable in this letter from Daniel about his "Granny."

Travels with Granny

They say you never really know a person until you've traveled with them. Well, I'm here to say that this is true, even when that person is your granny.

In 2011, Granny asked me to be her travel companion on a twelve-day river cruise from Moscow to St. Petersburg. It didn't take me long to say yes.

"Travels with Granny" turned out to be an experience, all right—and the fascinating history of Russia, with its beautiful vistas and landmarks, was only part of it. While the 250 fellow passengers were mostly an older crowd, Granny was actually the oldest person on the ship, and I was the youngest by far. We were definitely the "odd couple," sitting next to each other on every bus ride and at every meal, at the circus and at the ballet, and walking the cobblestoned streets with Granny's arm firmly clenching mine. And everybody had something to say about our relationship, from "I hope when my granddaughter is old enough, we'll travel together like the two of you!" to "My rotten

grandson would never go on a cruise with me—
he won't even go to a movie with me!"

Of course, we had our moments. Granny
routinely accosted people and asked them to
take our picture in front of every landmark in
Russia. But our travels brought Granny and me
closer than ever and created wonderful memories.
And thanks to her, I've got photographs of every
single one of them.

Daniel Negrin (26)
Livingston, New Jersey

In my case, it was my granddaughter Kathryn who
unknowingly made the first overture for me to enter her
world. Here's what I call my not-so-quiet wake-up call.

I was visiting my daughter Ellen and her family, and
I volunteered to pick up her younger daughter, Kathryn,
then thirteen, at the end of her school day.

"So, how was school?" I asked, by rote.

This time, Kathryn refused to give me a rote answer.
She deposited her backpack onto the ground and
resolutely folded her arms. "Grandpa," she said sharply,
"I'm *more* than just a student, you know!"

Of *course* I knew! But did I really know?

I knew that Kathryn's world went beyond the

academic subjects scribbled on her binder covers, and beyond the soccer games I'd inquire about diligently. She had a rich, deepening life of the mind, full of dreams and convictions, doubts, and fears, and now she was inviting me to enter her world through a small window *that might soon close.* So, I gave the only response I could.

"Thank you, Kathryn. I want to know more about you. And I want you to know more about me."

Standard queries, preachy advice, a check in the mail for birthdays and holidays—these weren't the tickets for admission into Kathryn's world. "I'm more than just a student, *Grandpa!*" It was, on the face of it, a gentle nudge, the words of a young teen who, even though she was grumpy after a tiring day, cared enough to try to tell me something.

It hit its mark like a laser. Kathryn then fell into silence. But my inner voice was shouting loud and clear. I didn't know her ideas about life, what music she liked, who her friends were, or how she felt about becoming a teenager. I knew it was time to act. But how? Reading and singing together, drinking the rain, and eating ice cream before dinner (shh, don't tell!), catching frogs, growing herbs, making paper airplanes and spaghetti and messes. These were the things that had filled us both with delight and amazement for years. But now she was a teenager, soon to be a young woman.

I needed a formula for inspiring the grandparent-grandchild connection beyond the "little kid" stage. It was all about the dinosaurs in kindergarten. Then suddenly the adults in their lives were expected to know the capitals of all fifty states. Next it was the night sky and constellations. After that, they were suddenly too busy with their own activities.

How to Enter Their World

How can you place value on what your grandchildren value? That's the ticket to open doors. When you live close to your grandchildren, you may have more of a handle on what their day-to-day interests are. But you can make the effort even from afar.

Is it "work" to truly enter the world of your grandchildren, to leave your comfort zone and try to understand another person from their perspective? Sometimes—like most things worth having—it is. Based on my experiences as a trained MSW clinician, however, I'd like to propose one word: *try*. The reality is that no matter how diligently we work on our relationships, none of them come with guarantees. Ultimately, there may be only modest ripples of change within your family. What I *can* promise unequivocally is that the very act of *trying* to be a more conscious, involved, sharing grandparent will enhance your well-being, and quell a good deal of whatever loneliness or disconnectedness you may experience.

And let's not forget about having fun. When entering each other's world, you can see how memorable experiences don't necessarily require lots of money. Furthermore, wonderful relationships aren't necessarily the product of lots of time with each other but making the most of the time you do have together.

Do we have to study the things our grandchildren are interested in? Yes, we do. And if you ask my friend Samuella, affectionately called Grandma Sammy by her family, she will tell you that time invested in learning about things your grandchildren are interested in is worth every minute. As with many grandparents, Sammy had noticed the difference as her grandson grew up. He went from that bouncy excitement of time with Grandma and Grandpa, relishing outings to train museums and getting root beer floats, to one-word, mostly grunted responses. It began around age twelve. Sammy took the "if you can't beat 'em, join 'em" approach to know more about his world. Here's Sammy's story told through the eyes of her daughter, Dana.

Grandma's Homework: Reading the Sports Page

I was sitting in Fitz's Restaurant in St. Louis when I overheard my mother, Sammy, getting a cherished one-on-one minute with my fifteen-year-old son, an avid St. Louis Blues hockey fan.

"So, how do you think the Blues will do with Elliott

gone?" Sammy asked. I knew my mother hated hockey, so I was surprised by her question.

"They'll do okay with the new goalie coming on," my son answered.

"You mean Allen? Do you think he'll stay?" Sammy asked by way of an actual sports-related follow-up question. This was blooming into a full-blown conversation between a grandparent and her teenage grandchild.

"Yeah," he answered. "And Hutton will be a good backup too."

Later that night, I couldn't help but comment. "Wow, Mom, that was impressive. You really studied!"

Sammy beamed with pride. "Yes, I now read the sports page!" she said, including an expletive for comedic effect. "The conversations are harder in person . . . I have to remember the names. At least if I'm on the phone I can just read from the newspaper." Preparing to see her grandson was like cramming for a test, to the point of having cheat sheets, but it was paying off.

Sammy learned that to engage with her grandchild, she needed to enter his world. And his world, based on his interests, was hockey: the game and the players. It took work on her part, but the resulting connection was so much more satisfying.

Our reality is framed by so many different things. And, yes, reality is subjective. You only need to think of your own childhood. For me, that started pre-television. Now, my grandchildren can carry a device and watch anything they want on demand, whenever and wherever they want. My grandchildren and I do live in different worlds. Both are wonderfully exciting and enriching. Both are informed by major world events of our formative years, pop culture and style, music, and modes of technology for communication. In my era, I would lift the receiver on a single phone that served an entire building and ask an operator to connect me to whomever I was calling. My grandchildren can say "Call Grandpa" out loud to an empty room and my phone will ring.

To enter someone else's world means taking off your own metaphorical glasses and putting on theirs, non-judgmentally, to see what they like, their views, and their day-to-day experiences.

Intergenerational Sharing

Generational names and years are "social constructs" that journalists, historians, and others have created to describe social trends. Note that different sources may use different years or attribute varying characteristics to each group. The groups are included here not to create stereotypes but to give a general idea of generational shifts and to provide context, with generational names you may recognize.

Traditionalists (born 1922–1945) are sometimes called the Silent Generation. According to *TIME* magazine, this term comes from the focus on careers over activism.[2] Baby boomers (born 1946–1964) were born into an era of optimism at the end of World War II and grew up during a time of healthy economic growth. Generation X (born 1965–1980), characterized by their cynical pessimism, is sometimes called the Forgotten Generation, as they are lost between the louder boomers and Generation Y. More popularly known as "millennials" (born 1981–2000), Generation Y strives for work-life balance, meaningful careers, and worries over footing the bill for Social Security now that boomers are retiring.[3] Generation Z, also called "NextGen," typically applies to those born after 2000 and is the first generation of digital natives, having grown up with technology. They also grew up under the constant threat of terrorism, just babies on September 11, 2001. And today's toddlers are in a generation that hasn't been named yet, given the fact that we are twenty years into NextGen.

The point is that each generation has its own set of challenges and influences. It's helpful to understand these impacts to be able to appreciate and support one

---

2 "The Silent Generation Revisited," *TIME*, June 29, 1970, http:// content.time.com/time/subscriber/article/0,33009,878847,00.html/.

3 "Generational Differences Chart," West Midland Family Center, last updated 2017. http://wmfc.org/uploads/GenerationalDifferen-cesChart.pdf/.

another. What we see with so many generations living together is a shift in how to judge aging. The categories used to be child (under 21), adult (21–60), and old (over 60). People are living longer, and many over eighty continue to be active and involved. The boomers, who are now 55–75, are starting new careers out of necessity with economic downturns, but also because they still have a lot to contribute.

One thing that really impacts each generation is what's happening in pop culture. Pop culture includes the things talked about with friends at school, whether that's your grandchildren today, or what happened at your school decades ago. How can you start to get to know what the other person is like when there is such a huge age gap? Music, politics, film, and television all offer points of entry to connect with each other.

My granddaughter and I started with music. She gave me a CD of one of her favorite groups that I listened to at home. I told her one of my favorite groups was the Weavers so she could listen on YouTube, Spotify, or another online music or video streaming service. The music exchange is one that can happen at any age. We each decided to stick with our own music. In fact, she called mine "interesting," which is often a euphemism for not wanting to offend someone. But in terms of the lyrics, it was truly fascinating to hear common themes of love, rejection, loneliness, and fun. These topics were the same, whether the music was from last year or last century.

For teenagers, you can have more thought-provoking exchanges around world events. Start by asking your grandchildren what events have impacted their ideas about the world. At the time of this writing, COVID-19, the #MeToo and Black Lives Matter movements, and gun violence were top of mind. What are some of the events that had you worried when you were their age? When I was sixteen and yearning to get my first car, I was also anxious about World War II and the first atomic bomb attack. By the time my son was sixteen, he worried about Vietnam and the draft. Not that all world events are ones to cause anxiety, but you may share something in common. Understanding the events that influence your grandchild's, or even your adult child's, worldview can lead to compassion. Maybe they are a little more anxious these days. You can feel compassion remembering your own experiences at their age.

All you need is some time together and a smartphone for the sharing to begin.

How to Enter Your Grandchild's World at School

As my grandchildren got older, it became clear that maintaining strong connections was increasingly challenging as their schedules grew more demanding and their academics, extracurriculars, and friendships predominated. The high school years are a critical period during which close bonds with caring family members are more important than ever. This is a time when our grandchildren are demanding autonomy and privacy, but they may also be grappling with issues that can be intensely overwhelming: challenging new academic undertakings, social pressures, cyberbullying, learning to drive, first-time employment, drug and alcohol abuse, sexual behavior, and gender-identity issues, to name just a few. You want to help, but you must get in the door first.

One doorway is to enter their world at school. Knowing what is happening in their world at their school creates context for discussion. You can visit their school's website to keep abreast of what is going on in their school community, regardless of how far away you live or whether their school is taking place remotely or in person in response to the COVID pandemic and its variants. This is absolutely true for high school websites. But don't stop after high school. College websites may have a stronger focus on recruitment, but they will give you a glimpse of campus life. High school and college newspapers, especially the opinion pages, can tell you the struggles and challenges your grandchild might be facing.

You can get their reading lists to read the books they're reading and ask for copies of the papers they write. My grandson Aidan gave me his seventh-grade reading list so I could read some of the books too. Not only did I have the enjoyment of revisiting some classics from my own youth, but I discovered some new classics as well. Aidan and I can have stimulating conversations about literature among other things. Imagine how wonderful and deep those conversations are at the college level.

My granddaughter Merete shared with us the step-by-step process of learning to read from a Torah scroll for her bat mitzvah. As a freshman in college, she sent me her papers to read. And my grandson Ethan, now an adult and an ordained rabbi, shares copies of his sermons with me. In fact, thanks to technology and livestreaming, I can watch him deliver his sermons in real time. That's a benefit of visiting the website where my grandchild works.

Early on, I realized how meaningful it was for me to get a feeling for what my grandchildren's lives were like at school, where they spent the bulk of their time. Recognizing that these years are such critical ones for young people, I approached the administration of the local public school, Deerfield High, with an idea to create a "Grandparents Orientation Day" as part of its annual back-to-school programming. I couldn't have hoped for a more enthusiastic buy-in from the school's administration. Grandparents shadow their grandchild to classes, and they learn from administrators about academics, clubs, and school safety. The guidance coun-selor helps grandparents understand what's happening at different ages and stages in their grandchild's social and emotional development.

Whether or not it would benefit your own grand-children, if volunteerism is in your blood, you might consider approaching a high school in your area to see if they would be interested in launching such a program, whether it be virtual or in person. Becoming involved in your local school system or in an organization that promotes intergenerational activities is an excellent in-vestment in a stronger and more connected community. And nothing keeps you young like being around young people!

Letters from Grandchildren: What I Learned from My Grandparent

Just as you work to learn about your grandchild's world, don't forget to share your own. For me, camping has been a lifelong theme. I was seventeen when I got my first job at a summer camp. I created a camp for children of US soldiers, officers, and military personnel when I was stationed in Japan during World War II. Back in the States after the war, I went from being a camp counselor to becoming director of an overnight camp. When my son asked how I wanted my family to celebrate my death, I told him to send me off in a canoe coffin. (I looked it up, they exist!) Camp is in my blood. It's at the core of my world.

Entering our grandchild's world means allowing them to make the choices that are right for them. And we are there to appreciate them, support them, and love them. Inviting your grandchildren into your world can inspire lessons that endure for a lifetime. That is powerfully apparent in these letters, written by grandchildren, about what they learned from their grandparents. The first letter is from my granddaughter Jessica. How wonderful to see that inviting her to share my world had an impact.

Camping with Grandpa

Camp has always been a very special place for my family. Growing up, it was my home away from home. I truly believe that my love for nature and wildlife began at camp.

One special thing that my grandfather and I would do together at camp was waking up before sunrise to watch the deer. We would walk to the lake and quietly observe the deer drinking from the lake as the sun rose. It was always a spectacular sight. I learned that sometimes you can take enormous pleasure in the most basic aspects of nature and life.

My favorite lesson that I learned from my grandfather at camp is to "always leave your campsite better than you found it." If you are camping and you see trash on the ground, pick it up and throw it out. Even if it's not yours, it's not a difficult thing to do and it makes a huge difference restoring the natural beauty of the land.

Love, Jessica (written at 28)
Los Angeles, California

Never a Word in Anger

My work for a judge requires me to read probation reports that detail a convict's life. These reports seem to teach that evil produces evil. Burglars often knew poverty as children. Drug users had the poison forced on them. Murderers, invariably, were abused as children.

So how is it, then, that my maternal grandmother, Rita Friedman (1928–2010), so thoroughly defied this apparent law of human nature to emerge a spirit of grace, humility, sweetness, and elegance? She was raised in Stalin's Russia. She endured a cruel stepfather.

Her studies were interrupted by Hitler's invasion of the Ukraine; she was evacuated east, but much of her family was executed by Nazis behind a tractor factory in Kharkov. All before she was twenty years old.

Yet none of us ever heard her speak a word in anger or resentment. Her delight was to encourage us in honorable pursuits; our delight was to present her with the fruits of that encouragement. I was eight when she first gave me a pen to chronicle our long, happy summers together in Vineland, New Jersey. From that day on, through my schooling and work as a journalist, until the hour of her death, I sent her not only every item I wrote, but every note I received in response.

She was an angel to us in life and is one now. Her memory reminds me every day that happiness is not the consequence of facts around us, but a state of soul within—and it is a choice.

Joseph F. Tartakovsky (31)
San Francisco, California

Your Turn: Journaling Expeditions

1. Make a list with your favorite music, favorite movie, the world event that most impacted your life, and/or the fashion trend that looked best on you. Add a second column for your grandchild to fill in their favorites. Fill out this grid and share the answers with each other. See each other's favorite movie together. Listen to each other's favorite music. (Pro-tip: Enjoy a dish of ice cream together as you work through the grid.) To download a copy of this chart, visit https://www.grandparentsunleashed.com/worlds-meet-resources/

Favorite	Grandparent	Grandchild
Music		
World event		
Books		
Games		
Movies		
Fashion		
Technology		

2. Visit the website for your grandchild's school. If you're not sure how to get there, ask your grandchild to show you when you are together. Select and write down three actions you will take based on the information you find. For example, identify a school event to attend. Watch a video or livestream from the website. Pick a book to read from their reading list. These are the types of things that you might be inspired to do by perusing the school website.

3. Put your intentions in writing. If you plan to ask to read one of their school papers or assignments, write down a deadline by when you will do it, and stick to it.

4. Write down three to five open-ended questions that could start a conversation about world views. For example, "Is college still worth the investment?" "What do you see as injustices in your community and how would you go about changing them?" Invite your grandchild's parents to join in the conversation. These questions probe generational views on current ideas, issues, and trends.

CHAPTER 3

Tell Stories

Stories are a superpower that bring generations together around shared experiences. The stories that endure can make up a family's history. As a grandparent, you can use stories to make your family history come alive. Perhaps you want to relay something funny to entertain. You can use stories to teach a lesson. That said, stories are *not* about preaching. Nor are stories inherently requests for advice or solutions. Of course, as a grandparent, you want to teach lessons. But stories are an opening for mutual sharing. Stories are a gateway for you and your grandchild to enter each other's world.

How can you prompt your grandchildren to tell stories? Try forgoing the traditional questions: *How are you? How was school? What did you learn in school today?* These questions most often elicit a one-word response: "Fine." Or maybe a grunt. Try instead: "Tell me a story about school today." Or first share a story of your own to get the ball rolling, like Eva's grandmother did, as her granddaughter shares in this letter.

Activism, Inspired by a Grandmother

About a dozen years ago—when I was a middle-school student, like those I currently teach—my grandmother began sharing with me the details of her own teenage years. During the Holocaust, she was one of nearly thirty thousand "Partisans." The Partisans were Jewish and Russian fighters who resisted the Nazis and banded together in the Polish forests. As Grandma Sonia opened up, so did my whole world.

Despite our lives having been so different on the surface, I know that my grandmother had felt many of the same things I felt as a young woman going out into the world: growing out of girlhood shyness, leaving a protected family cocoon, and experiencing the first stirrings of romance. Today, I find myself struggling to understand her frame of mind at two distinct life-junctures: that of the courageous teenager who fought for survival, and that of the eighty-seven-year-old woman who has come so far and is surrounded by people who love and admire her, yet who at times feels utterly alone and empty, as one of so few survivors.

Grandma bravely wrote and published a memoir several years ago titled, Here, There Are No Sarahs. There's a story in it I've known since childhood, and it always stuck with me. During the first bitter cold winter that her family hid in the Polish forest, they were extremely depressed—huddled together for warmth and hardly speaking, knowing they were being hunted and their lives were in danger. A Ukrainian peasant named Tichon came upon them. He could have abandoned them or even turned them over to the Nazis. Instead, when he saw sixteen-year-old Sonia, he started to cry. "You older folks at least have had a chance to live," he said, "but why does that young girl have to suffer? What sin did she commit?"[4] Tichon became instrumental in the survival of Sonia and her family, bringing them desperately needed food, information, and hope. My grandmother's grateful recounting of this humble man's heroic acts taught me that each of us has the power to stand up against evil and injustice by helping those in need.

---

4 Sonia Shainwald Orbuch, *Here, There Are No Sarahs* (Columbus, OH: Gatekeeper Press, 2009), 70.

As I've grown into adulthood, the more I have learned about my grandmother's unexpected role as a resistance fighter, the more I feel the mandate to carry on her spirit. Clearly, she was fighting for her life, and I fight for justice and human rights because I have the luxury to do so. Still, I believe that we are guided by the same truths, encapsulated in the words of Dr. Martin Luther King Jr.: "Injustice anywhere is a threat to justice everywhere." My grandmother's story was part of what inspired me to my current work as a teacher in a public school in a seriously disadvantaged neighborhood.

We live in a world where injustice and bigotry, persecution, and genocide have still not been conquered. Sometimes this feels overwhelming. But I know I will always find strength and inspiration to keep doing my small part when I think of my grandmother—the strongest woman I know.

Eva Orbuch (23)
San Jose, California

A story has amazing power to connect across the generations. My son, Michael, is an accomplished child psychiatrist. He says, "It is more natural for youth to speak in terms of stories than in terms of feelings, evaluations, thoughts, and plans." He acknowledges that while this changes as people mature, sometimes getting our grandchildren talking is about finding the right place or opening with a point of empathy.

When my granddaughter Merete was in high school, I wanted to get an idea of what was happening along the lines of bullying. I broached the topic by sharing a story about a time when I was bullied at school. When I was in sixth grade, I had the great honor of being a patrol boy. I wore a special belt. My job was to protect my fellow classmates to safely cross the street on their way into school. One day, two girls started to cross the street. I told them to stop until the light changed and it was safe to cross, but they didn't stop. So I told the principal.

After school, four boys approached me. One of them said, "You reported my girlfriend to the principal?"

"Yes, she was endangering herself. I report that," I retorted.

With that, he and his friends started to beat me up.

Two patrol boys who were standing nearby saw the fight. "Leave him alone! He was right!" they said as the bullies backed away. The boy and his friends were picking on me because I had done the right thing. But most importantly, I felt the support and compassion of the boys who intervened.

I was reminded of the patrol boy story when my granddaughter Merete told me about how she supported a friend who was being cyberbullied at school. Some kids were passing around a picture of her friend saying she was a "pig." Merete saw the girl after school, alone and sad, and went to comfort her.

Two stories, seventy years apart. But the stories are connected over time and space by compassion and similarity in how upstanders can make a difference when someone is being bullied. If I had asked Merete, "Why are you sad?" she likely would have said, "I don't want to talk about it, Grandpa." Instead, through our stories we had a meaningful discussion.

What Makes a Good Story?

When it comes to our grandchildren, we relish every word they say. I, however, have found that to keep a grandchild's attention, there is great value in practicing stories and following some tips essential for good storytelling. Here are a few things to think about when crafting the stories you will tell.

1. **Every story has a beginning, a middle, and an end**

   Think of it like a big hill. The story starts, it rises to

the biggest point at the top, and then comes down and ends on the other side.

2. **Decide where you will start to grab attention right away**
   If the story is about how you got a speeding ticket at 5:00 p.m., you probably don't need to start with what you had for breakfast that morning. Perhaps the beginning is when you got into the car, or it might even be when you got onto the highway. It could look something like this: "I was on my way to pick you up from school. I guess I was driving a little fast when I got onto the highway. Then this happened. Then that happened. And in the end, that's why I was late to pick you up from practice today."

3. **A good story should be about one thing**
   The story might be about the day you and your spouse got married. It could be the story of how you met your spouse, or when your first child was born. These are each separate and distinct stories. It's easy to get sidetracked and insert one story into another, but staying focused on the single story will make it more engaging and memorable.

What Makes a Good Listener?

In telling your stories there is an implied invitation to

your grandchildren to share stories of their own. An important part of sharing stories is to be a good listener, including listening to the silences. My son the psychiatrist says that when a grandchild is telling a story, the silences tell you what is hard for them to talk about. Silences tell you when you can ask a clarifying question. They tell you if the story is done.

Be very careful about inserting solutions or best-case endings or the content of your catastrophic worrying. And try not to react to details that concern you but are not part of the story. For example, your grandchild may want to share an adventure that happened during sixth period at school. If you jump on the revelation that they clearly skipped school, you will never get the story. You will more likely hear "Never mind" or "You don't understand." And that's the last thing you want when your grandchild finally shares a story with you. Your concern about the detail is valid, but you may want to pick another time to address it. Remember, it's *their* story. Don't insert a new ending to show how you would have handled it. (Unless, of course, they asked you what you would have done in that situation!)

How can you tell if your grandchild is listening? Look for eye contact and facial expressions. You can ask for understanding. For example, you could say, "Can you imagine what that was like?" or "Can you picture it?" You also may want to ask before starting a story if they have time, as in, "Do you have time for a quick story?" Another idea for engagement is to connect your story to what your grandchild is saying. I've used "Thank you for sharing with me what happened. I had a similar experience when I was your age . . ." Just be sure to remember your own good listening skills. You don't want to shift focus from your grandchild to you if they are sharing something sensitive. Follow the conversation where it goes. If your grandchild seems distracted, ask them what's on their mind, and save your story for another time. You can always use the current moment to schedule when you will get together again.

The Best Places to Jumpstart Storytelling

Sharing stories when your grandchildren are young is a way to build the habit. Afterall, when they are younger, they often can't wait to tell you stories about everything! Even the smallest event could be a long and detailed story. However, if you have never tried storytelling and are starting now with your teenage grandchildren, there's no need to fret. My son, Michael, acknowledges that while this ease of storytelling changes as youths age, sometimes getting them talking is about finding the right place. Here are some places he recommends.

1. **In the car (especially if both the listener and speaker are in the front seat)**

"Side-by-side sitting normalizes and democratizes the roles in the storytelling," says Michael. It conveys the idea that both grandchild and grandparent are in this journey together with no active power differential.

Plus, you get the added benefit of helping your adult children by offering to drive your grandchildren to or from practice or other events. Sometimes it's the in-between times, not the big events, where connection can happen.

2. **On a walk**

   Taking a walk together is another way to plan for some side-by-side time. It allows a grandchild to avoid direct eye contact, which Michael says can be "misconstrued as a threat (more likely with boys) or a criticism (more likely with girls)."

3. **At a restaurant or the kitchen table**

   If you get a chance to share a meal or a beverage together, sit kitty-corner rather than across from each other. Do it even if that means foregoing the booth in favor of a table. Strategically, that allows for selective use of direct eye contact. Plus, food is nurturing and encourages colorful conversation.

4. **While doing "chores" together**

   Think of things like washing the car, cooking, or

grocery shopping together. The car washing can inspire fun play. Cooking has the reward of sharing something delicious when it's ready. Grocery shopping allows for car time on the way to and from the store. Plus, it's a fun way to see what your grandchild likes to eat these days. That's how I found out one grandchild was now vegan. That's important to know if you are planning to have dinner out together![5]

Keep a Story Bowl

What do you want to know about your grandchildren? And what stories do you want to tell them about yourself? Sometimes it can be hard to think of the perfect story to make a connection, to share empathy with your grandchild, and to normalize what they are experiencing.

One idea is to keep a story bowl. All you need are index cards or Post-It notes, or a Google Doc for those who are more internet savvy, something to write with, and a bowl. As you think of topics for stories, things you would like to know about your grandchildren, or

---

5 An earlier draft of this content was previously published as "Grandchildren: Places and Spaces to Inspire Sharing Stories," *Grand: Living the Ageless Life*, May 23, 2019, https://www.grandmagazine. com/2019/05/grandchildren-places-and-spaces-to-inspire-sharing-stories/.

experiences you would like to share, write them on a slip of paper and put them into your story bowl.

For example, you could write down what books you used to read as a child when you would hide under the covers at night with a flashlight. What did your childhood bedroom look like? Or recall a time when you were the most scared. Or a social issue that drove you to action. When you and your grandchild are together, you can each pick a slip of paper from the story bowl and tell each other a story based on that prompt idea.

What stories will your grandchildren tell their grandchildren? Which stories will stick? Which ones become the lore of family from generation to generation? We just never know. But I do know that now is the time to share stories, for the moment's joy of sharing memories and as a doorway to meaningful conversation.

Letters from Grandchildren: What I Learned from My Grandparent

Our grandchildren may remember more stories than you can ever imagine. Jacob, for example, recalls his grandfather's stories about life in Auschwitz that have remained with him in adulthood.

The Mantle of Storytelling

Zeyde was always a storyteller. Throughout

my child-hood, stories trickled out of him, and
sometimes out of his children, in unpredictable
times and places. Stories of the frigid Christmas
in Auschwitz, when he siphoned piles of apple
and potato peels from the kitchen of a Nazi
officers' feast to the barracks of his starving
friends. Stories of New Year's Eve, 1946, when
Zeyde danced with a beautiful woman at a party
in a Displaced Persons camp—the same woman
he had spotted in a soup line immediately after
the camps were liberated. Zeyde and Bubbi held
fast to each other for the next fifty years.

Zeyde made me a storyteller too. I wrote
about him in my college essay, and he is the
wise, tenacious grandfather who always finds
his way into my fiction. I shared his tales before
a group of fifty teenagers in the barracks of
Auschwitz-Birkenau sixty-five years after he'd
slept there. I told them how he smiled like a
constellation of faraway stars as he described
the faces of prisoners who watched him on that
Christmas night wheel in a wheelbarrow, remove
a tarp, then some tools, and then a mini-Everest
of apple and potato peels.

Now, at ninety-two, the man still has pleasures. Recently, over a game of five-card stud, he beckoned me to the bottles of Courvoisier he secretes in a cabinet near the front door. "You want something real nice to drink, Jacob? It goes down..." And he held the air with his hand and pursed his lips to indicate an immaculate smoothness.

"What are you talking about in there, Mr. Kaufman?" his aide, Jill, called coyly from the other room. He gave me another one of those smiles that could illuminate the world as he raised his teacup with an "ahhhh." If my parents hadn't summoned me to leave just then, I'm pretty sure that Zeyde would have offered his usual toast—"I'm gonna tell you, everyone shall be healthy, we will be here, next year, together . . . L'chaim!"—and the two of us would have gotten good and drunk together.

In the car my dad asked what had prompted Zeyde to dip into the Courvoisier and to reveal his stash to me. I didn't have an answer. "The whole thing was pretty spontaneous," I said. My mother said, "Maybe he was remembering some night of drunken revelry and poker in the bungalow colony we stayed at when I was a kid." Or maybe he was remembering the night of the dance when he captured his dream girl.

Every time I retell his stories, every time his words spill from my lips, they play out slightly differently: some details are lost, a few are embellished, and some are just wrong. In part, I'm pained by this, but I'll bet Zeyde never told the exact same story twice either. I think that's just how people keep stories alive.

Jacob Kose (23)
New York, New York

Letters from Grandchildren: Food Edition

Food is a cornerstone of tradition. Often recipes are passed from generation to generation. No matter how "modern" grandparenting becomes, nothing can replace the smells, the tastes, and the shared treats of time spent with grandparents. If you are having a hard time thinking of stories to tell, start with a favorite dish. The smell of a certain food can bring back the most vivid memories of times shared with grandchildren.

Pancakes

My grandmother made me pancakes whenever I visited her. Without fail, I would arrive to the smell of hot butter and the sight of a yellow Bisquick box on the kitchen counter. Even if I wasn't hungry, she would sit me down for a heaping plate. Every time.

Grandma Mimi knew what I didn't: that I desperately needed something dependable in my life. I was seven, and my parents' divorce had shaken my family and left them both helpless. I believe I could have been driven into terrible habits or a hopeless future. But she gave me the semblance of a strong foundation, even if I saw her no more than once a month.

Those pancakes became something to look forward to, a glint of hope in a wider story of despair. Grandma Mimi and her pancakes provided me with the stability I needed, something warm and nourishing in days that felt dark and cold.

Jesse J. Rabbits (22)
Harrisburg, Pennsylvania

Persian Cooking to Comfort the Heart in Exile

Eshagh Abdollahzadeh spent the first sixty-two years of his life living comfortably in Tehran, buying and selling real estate, and providing heavy machinery for roadwork to subcontractors of the Shah.

The hardest decision of his life was uprooting his wife and children to America following the 1979 Islamic Revolution. As Jews, they were forced to seek religious asylum.

Living on Long Island, my grandmother said of her husband, "Esi suffered the way exiles suffer—he left part of his heart in Iran."

Friday nights at my grandparents' house was a tradition and where I hold my most precious memories with Esi. The complex aromas of traditional Persian cooking would awaken my taste buds the moment I walked through the door.

We shared a love for my grandma's traditional Persian-style cooking. Friday night meant ab goosht (Jewish chicken soup) and gondi (Persian matzah balls), tadig (Persian crispy rice), and Esi's favorite, khoresht gheymeh, Persian stew with yellow peas.

"Pari, put a little khoresht on my rice," he would tell my grandma. "No goosht [meat]."

Esi took his health seriously and stopped eating red meat after coming to America. He never ate in restaurants and stuck to a diet of whatever Persian food my grandmother cooked.

It was all he needed. It tasted like home.

Jessica Khorsandi (20)
Great Neck, New York

Chocolate, A World Away

My grandfather spoke some English, but not much. I speak some Hindi, but not much. But we both loved chocolate.

When I would visit him in New Delhi once a year, we made it a ritual to buy a bag of chocolate and just sit together—sometimes in silence, sometimes engaging in halting small talk. It was peaceful. Joyous.

At times I felt like I was missing out. He wasn't the sort of grandfather who I could sit and talk to for hours, who gave me sage advice on life and love. All we did was eat sweets and watch television.

Since he passed away, though, I can never eat a piece of chocolate without thinking about him and his smile. Those moments mean the most to me today. I would do anything to be with him enjoying a Hershey's Kiss.

Priya Vij (21)
Houston, Texas

Your Turn: Journaling Expeditions

1. Is there an anecdote you recall that encapsulates your own grandparent's legacy? What lesson(s) did you take from this story at the time? And today, in hindsight, do you see it differently? If so, how?

2. Write a list of some "first" stories to exchange with your grandchild. The subject can vary based on their age. For example, tell each other the story of learning to ride a bike, the story of your first date, or the story of your first job. Separated by decades, these stories of mutual "firsts" will melt the years between you.

3. What's something that you wish your grandchild would talk to you about? What's a story that you can share first to get the ball rolling? Write it down.

4. What's a food item or dish that carries special meaning for you? Is it something you can share with your grandchild? What's a nostalgic food from your childhood? Perhaps you have the original recipe or can find one online that's similar. Make it together and share the story about it.

CHAPTER 4

Give Voice to Your Values

Grandparents often ask me, "How will I be remembered?" You can leave valuables to your loved ones, but things can be lost, discarded, or no longer considered valuable. A legacy of values, however, can guide grandchildren in their daily life, school, friendships, and family relationships. A value such as caring becomes integrated into the being of the grandchild's personality. It can be forever, and it can be shared and taught to other members of the family and friends. It is part of the sharing culture of the family, and the grandchild's world outside of the family. And have no doubt: *It is within your power* to leave your family with greater meaning and to leave the world a better place because your family was in it.

The simplest definition of a *value* is something you believe in—a belief system—that guides your priorities when taking action in life. Every member of your family can determine what those values are. The purpose is to talk about how to share values together and among family members. My granddaughter Kathryn expresses her thoughts on the topic in this letter that she wrote to me.

Keep Your Eye on the Ball

I remember it like it was yesterday—the times I spent in downtown Chicago in my grandparents' old apartment. I remember family dinners, I remember playing dominos in the living room, and I remember my grandparents' cooking. I remember "swimming" in my grandmother's "messy room." However, of all the memories, what I remember the most is playing catch with my grandpa in his back room. It felt like hours were spent back there with a package of tennis balls, and my grandpa repeating one line: "Kathryn, always keep your eye on the ball!"

I enjoyed playing catch, and as I grew older, I played softball, soccer, and basketball—and through the years my grandpa would continue telling me to keep my eye on the ball. No matter what sport it is, you have to be determined and stay focused.

Well, I soon learned that keeping your eye on the ball did not only have to be about a tennis or soccer ball but was a way of thinking about life and keeping focused on anything you wanted. If you want something enough, you need to work hard and keep track of the objective no matter what it is.

As great as all the memories are, when asked to put in writing what I have learned from my grandparents, I wanted to be sure to do it justice by expressing the impact of their unconditional love. This love they have given me and the rest of our family is a foundation to live a happy, healthy life . . . no matter what our road or how curvy it may be along the way. What I carry with me the most from my grandparents is fairly simple: to be a good person and a good family member, and to play an active role in every community I am a part of.

Love,
Kathryn (written at 25)

Family Values: What Do You Stand for and Why?

What do you and your family stand for? The process of sharing our values with our grandchildren starts the day they are born. Values are visible in what we say and even more so in our actions. There are many ways to teach values. You can teach them by discussion—simply telling someone what you believe in. You can share them in writing. You can also share your values by example. You may go to church every week to demonstrate your commitment to spirituality and invite your grandchildren to tag along. One grandma I know is a vegetarian and serves only plant-based dishes when family visits. She leaves pamphlets about factory farming on pillows as her special turndown service when her grandchildren spent the night. Granted, this is not so subtle, but it does have her adult children and grandchildren discussing not only this specific value, but the idea of values and how different people believe different things.

As a grandparent, we only have so much influence on our grandchildren's values. Everyone's experience of the world supports and challenges their beliefs, and that is constant across the lifespan. While values may be based on where or how you were raised, even siblings who grow up in the same house and have the same parents may believe entirely different things.

In the future, your grandchildren may be partnered and building their own family values, balancing what each brings to this new family pod. Don't underestimate the influence of culture on values, which comes into play as more and more families are interfaith and intercultural. What's wonderful is to have instilled the importance of values and the ability to identify and articulate one's values that your grandchildren will bring with them into adulthood.

There's no guarantee as to which of our values will stick or which they will eschew outright. Sometimes, as our grandchildren grow up and engage with the world, their values may influence us. The process of communicating our values starts with turning values into action and conscientiously embodying our values through shared activities.

The Family Values Quiz

How do you discover family members' values? In our family, we started with what I hoped was a short, stimulating quiz, titled the Family Values Quiz.

I won't deny it. As one might expect, there was plenty of eye rolling when I announced to my family on a Thanksgiving weekend that it was time to turn off the TV, take a break from the leftovers and chit-chat, and convene in the living room. When I actually started distributing paper and pencils so everyone could fill out a Family Values Quiz, there were audible groans! Most of them went along with it, I've no doubt, solely to indulge good ol' Dad a.k.a. Grandpa. This didn't exactly thrill me, but I barreled ahead anyway. What kind of an example would I be if I didn't persevere when something really mattered to me?

The results of our Family Values Quiz highlighted some things I had already felt about how we interacted at our best. Discussing important topics like social justice, education, and religion was clearly a natural platform for our family, even its junior members. To give some structure to the conversation, I pre-filled the list of values in the first column with things that were important to me, or that I knew were important to other family members (even some who had passed away). I left some extra rows for write-ins.

The instructions are simple: Rate the importance of each value to you on a scale of one to five. And, if so inspired, suggest a potential activity that your family could do together that captured the essence of the value. Exact adherence to the "rules" here is not what is important. If this quiz leaves your family with a commitment to doing even one values-based activity together, I would view that as a success. To download a copy of this quiz, visit https://www.grandparentsunleashed.com/worlds-meet-resources/

Sample Family Values Quiz

Value Description	Importance Not at All Extremely					Potential Activity
	1	**2**	**3**	**4**	**5**	
Adventure (new experiences, challenges, excitement)	1	2	3	4	5	• Travel as a family. • Start a family adventure book club.
Contribution and Generosity (desire to make a difference, to give)	1	2	3	4	5	• Volunteer together.
Creativity and Artistic Expression (new ideas, innovation, experimenting, drama, painting, literature)	1	2	3	4	5	• Family trip to an art museum or the theater. • Go to a concert at a local college.
Economic Security (freedom from financial worries)	1	2	3	4	5	• Commitment to financially helping other family members when they need it. (It's a gift, not a loan).
Environmentalism (caring for the earth, nature)	1	2	3	4	5	• Participate in an Earth Day event. • Go hiking together.

Equity and Inclusion (embracing diverse cultures, equal chance, equal hearing for all)	1	2	3	4	5	• Host international visitors for special dinners. • Learn about another culture together. • Seek out cultural immersion opportunities. • Learn about social issues together. • Host a mock debate.
Friendship (intimacy, care, support)	1	2	3	4	5	• Schedule weekly Zoom calls. • Consistently call one another just because. • Create a family group chat.
Inner Harmony (desire to be at peace with oneself)	1	2	3	4	5	• Meditate together. • Send a breathing exercise to the family group chat.

Personal Development and Learning (improvement, reaching potential, growth, and knowledge)	1	2	3	4	5	• Participate in a Zoom study class. • Read each other's papers (from school). • Take turns teaching something to the rest of the family at Family Meetings.
Spirituality (belief or interest in a higher power or God)	1	2	3	4	5	• Pray together. • Go to a place of worship together, or any place that inspires awe (e.g., a botanical garden, the Grand Canyon, etc.) • Celebrate religious holidays together.
Interdependence (ability to ask for help and give help)	1	2	3	4	5	Bring up any needs and challenges at a Family Meeting.

The values in this sample quiz are suggestions, albeit ones that rose to the top for my family. Use this quiz as a starting point to fill in the values for you and your family. Some will be very concrete and easy to translate into activities. Other ideas might be a little more abstract, yet no less important. Some other ideas could be:

- **Cooperation** (teamwork, working with others)

- **Integrity** (honesty, sincerity, consistent demonstration of your values)

- **Fun** (enjoyment, pleasure, happiness)

- **Family Happiness** (desire to get along, respect, harmony)

Even if some of these feel too conceptual to build an activity around, they still offer a doorway for rich discussion. Which items to include on your personalized Family Values Quiz is a great agenda item for a Three-Generation Family Meeting (see Chapter 5). For us it worked to do the quiz in person. Google Docs, Survey Monkey, or other technology platforms are also options that may work for your family.

The quiz drove home that all of us appeared to relish both teaching and learning according to our individual abilities, knowledge, and interests. We didn't need to share the same passions or beliefs to be brought closer by them. We could grow, individually and as a unit, by talking about what it was we loved, by listening, asking questions, and demonstrating support.

Have fun taking the quiz, tallying the results, and discussing them. What will emerge is a kind of treasure map for your family life—a picture of the many rich attributes and values, interests, and convictions that each of you contributes to the collective to make it a vibrant whole. Keep in mind, this is not a test. Rather it's a thought-starter around possible values as a basis for discussion to see where values intersect, diverge, and overlap.

Keep Trying

In my programs and workshops with grandparents, some have said that they were not able to see the process of discussing values completely through. I have two suggestions for this. First, how about taking a reverse-engineering approach? That's where you start with the end goal—a shared activity—and work backward to the values discussion. It may be easier to schedule the activities first. Start with things that reflect your own values. Once you are together, make that connection. For example, "I invited you to watch *The Rachel Maddow Show* with me because I value being politically aware and acting in accordance with that. What do you believe in? Let's do your activity next time."

Secondly, you tried and you will still be ahead of where you were before. You'll have a picture, on paper, of your family's strongest shared values, favorite memories, and activities—an excellent jumping-off point for discussion and action. Repeating this exercise every three to four years is another way to see where you have been and where you are going, as the generational wheel steadily turns.

Navigating Disagreement

The goal of the values conversation is to find the values you have in common to deepen your connection. Values can be very personal. While your grandchildren may share some of your values, they will embrace values of their own as they become adults. It is likely that you will find topics on which you don't agree. Teenagers will disagree *just because* or to assert independence. (Remember, that's developmentally normative.)

Interestingly, delving into values often helps people discover unexpected areas of commonality, notwithstanding what may appear to be striking differences of opinion. Some families are very much split along political or ideological lines. There's nothing wrong with healthy disagreement and debate, of course—it's all part of a vibrant sharing culture. But if social justice emerges as a strong core value for all or most family members, there are ways to experience and manifest this together that are decidedly nonpartisan. Families can take on projects at the intersection of their values. For example, families across the political spectrum, or with different religious beliefs or practices, can volunteer together in a soup kitchen or for a community renewal project.

That said, you have to be able to express opposing opinions respectfully to find those intersections. Here are some tips to help navigate conversations, with the goal of understanding each other in mind.

- Always separate the person from the idea. You love the person even if you do not agree with their idea.

- Listen to what the person says to understand how he or she feels.

- Use positive and respectful language when discussing differences.

- In the end, you may agree to disagree. You may never come to agree on a particular subject.

It may help you to try and define your family ethos by zeroing in on shared interests or things that everyone likes to do together for fun and then connect the underlying values. This echoes the forementioned reverse-engineering approach. For example, family members who enjoy swimming may find that they share an affinity for environmental issues. A family that enjoys playing chess may be interested in strategy and how that informs politics and democracy. Families who have fun cooking together may find an underlying concern for food equity or supporting locally owned restaurants.

Remember that interests, hobbies, and activities, for a host of reasons, may wax and wane throughout the years. Core values, however, tend to endure, and they are frequently the foundation for our lasting passions and enthusiasms. A family with a core value of outdoor adventures and fitness may relish taking ski trips together each winter. But what happens during the years when money is tight or when a good portion of the family's members are either too old or too young to participate? The members who can no longer actively participate can still have fun together and fulfill the very same core value by going to watch their family sledding or ice-skating in a local park.

By exploring and coming to terms with our family's areas of commonality and separateness, we teach the youngest generation how people of different beliefs respect each other, value each other's contributions, and manage to get along in the world.

Values discussions may feel lofty, but the application of the spirit of the value can fit into a family's everyday conversations. Here's how one grandparent I know, Rebecca, broached the subject in her family.

Rebecca's Story: The Value of Adventure in Action

When Rebecca introduced the conversation around values with her family, both adventure and multiculturalism rose to the top as important.

At first Rebecca was discouraged, thinking the only

way to realize these values was to have lots of money to travel internationally. Instead, she and her grandchildren came up with a fun way to try new restaurants, new foods, and to learn about cultures different from their own.

First, they agreed that they would try a new restaurant every time they went out to eat together. Second, they made picking the restaurant a lesson in geography. À la pin the tail on the donkey, each would take a turn wearing a blindfold and be given a piece of tape to post on the big, laminated map that hung on the wall at Grandma Rebecca's house. Take away any markers that ended up in the middle of an ocean, and the resulting countries would give them choices as to where to eat. As a result, they have tried fast food from Pakistan, traditional dishes from Sri Lanka, and even met the Finance Minister of Kyrgyzstan who happened to be visiting and dining at the same restaurant on one of their outings.

Rebecca knew that diversity and multiculturalism went well beyond just food and festivals. Through the commitment to sharing values, however, she found ways to use those markers as a launching pad to delve deeper into cultural differences and to allow her and her grandchildren to connect with people from different backgrounds. That can be a start to combatting stereotypes and bias.

Many grandparents may live in smaller towns or cities where there is not such diversity of cultural representation. Luckily, the internet or even books from the library can offer alternatives. Virtual tours of other countries and even ethnic cookbooks and ingredients ordered online can be the basis for meaningful time spent together with grandchildren. The absence of difference is a prompt for a values discussion as well. What do we lose when a community is racially and ethnically homogenous? What are the historical or systemic influences on the makeup of a community? This is an extremely relevant conversation and connects the value of adventure to the values of diversity, equity, and inclusion.

Letters from Grandchildren: What I Learned from My Grandparent

Before we leave this discussion on values, I wanted to share this wonderful letter from Stephen, who, now nearing grandparenting age himself, still carries the lessons and values he learned from his grandmother.

Fighting Discrimination

Every time I open a bottle of Veuve Clicquot, I think of my paternal grandmother, not only because of her natural effervescence but because of her strong resemblance to Madame Clicquot, whose stoic image appears on the tiny metal cap above the cork.

Grandma Ethel also looked a little like George Washington. Unlike George, however, she didn't always tell the truth, but would instead embellish facts in such a clever, loving way as to steer the entire family into her way of thinking. For instance, Donald, the little boy who lived across the street from her, was never available for my cousin Pam and me to play with because, insisted Grandma, "He's in jail." (In fact, he was just a little too rough for her tastes.)

Ethel may have lived in Beverly Hills, but her protective instincts, especially where the children were concerned, hearkened back to her own childhood in Russia. "They wouldn't let us go to school," I can still hear her tell me, some thirty-three years after her death (peacefully, in her sleep, thankfully). It was understood who "they" were, and her words echo in my head every time I witness any sort of discrimination taking place against an individual or group. Was this her greatest gift? Possibly. Although, now in our sixties—and occasionally stuck for something to do—Pam and I will still turn to one another and ask with wide-eyed bemusement, "Do you think Donald is out of jail yet?"

Stephen M. Silverman (61)
New York, New York

Your Turn: Journaling Expeditions

1. Write down the three most important values for you personally. Can you rank them and share why they resonate for you so strongly?

2. Set a timer for ten minutes and write a story about an experience in your life that embodies one of the values you jotted down above.

3. Review your Family Values Quiz and group the activities in the Potential Activity column into two categories: ones that are fairly easily attained (e.g., "Start a family book club") to more complicated undertakings that are further in the future and would require more planning (e.g., "Take a family 'roots' trip to Ireland together").

4. If your family has not yet done the Family Values Quiz together, do it on your own and brainstorm

activity ideas. Doing the activity first, before the discussion, can also be a way to ignite conversation.

CHAPTER 5

Host Family Meetings

Families today can easily be in the same house and rarely see each other, let alone have meaningful conversations. Being supported and supportive in a family must go deeper than asking, "How are you?" It's even harder for grandparents who may not live in the same house nor the same city. We can't know what our grandchildren are facing or how they are feeling without conscientiously setting time to connect. Three-Generation Family Meetings, when scheduled regularly—twice a year in person at family gatherings, or more often with videoconferencing—are a way to guarantee that family is making time for each other and to truly explore what is going on in each family member's life.

Grandparents can take the lead to get this started. Many of us work or have worked in impactful and sometimes exciting professions—theater, art, music, education, medicine, law, business, and technology. We have created PowerPoint presentations and written mission statements. We have set goals, objectives, and benchmarks to measure success and then reevaluated and reset those goals and objectives.

When considering how to bring your strengths, wisdom, skills, and knowledge in guiding yourself and your family as well as enriching your family's life, these skills traditionally associated with the private and public sector professional world can have a profound and lasting impact.

As a business leader, my Family Meetings felt familiar. Yet taking this typical business fare and adapting it for my family changed the paradigm of how all three generations connected.

I proposed to my family that we set aside some time for a formalized Family Meeting during holiday celebrations. In this meeting, we spend a couple of hours with a planned agenda that includes guided discussion and almost always a snack or treat to enjoy. The two holidays we traditionally spend together—one religious, one secular—are both rife for the deeper interactions and relationship-building that a Family Meeting affords.

Thanksgiving is a natural juncture for everyone, youngest to oldest, to reflect on what we are thankful for, and on what we might wish for ourselves and for each other in the coming season. On the Jewish holiday of Passover, the centerpiece of the Seder dinner is the reading of the Haggadah: the annual retelling, "from generation to generation," of the ancient Hebrews' exodus from Egypt. Its epic themes of freedom, redemption, and renewal are a springboard for fascinating values-based discussions, both personal and political.

I admit that many attended our first Family Meeting a little begrudgingly, and mostly out of love and obligation to me, Grandpa. In fact, the first meeting lasted only thirty minutes, and I did all the talking. But I upheld the value of *trying*.

Nowadays, when I say, "Take out the pen and paper if you want to take notes, because it's time for our meeting," there is still a groan or two. But everyone participates and shares a story of success or hardship from the past six months or contributes agenda items for family discussion.

Did we engage in these kinds of discussions before undertaking Family Meetings? Sure we did. But coming up with carefully considered topics helped us to focus and enrich our all-too-rare time together. Even with the separation of family members because of the COVID-19 pandemic, and the regular use of Zoom to meet by videoconference, there is still nothing as powerful as meeting in person with no distractions. In fact, our family has had regular calls every Sunday for over a year. They are shorter and unplanned other than a set day and time, and different people show up each week. I treasure them, but not to replace our in-person Family Meeting.

Family Meetings also add an element of intimacy,

with the pre-meeting check-in for agenda items, and the implied invitation for deeper conversation after the meeting. I can seek out a family member to ask follow-up questions and give support and a much-needed hug whether they have shared a hardship or a reason to celebrate.

Maybe you can't make every initiative in this chapter get off the ground the first time. Maybe you won't get everybody's buy-in each and every time. Whatever you do accomplish, however, will be a big step in the direction of a more enriching family connection. Every suggestion in this chapter about agenda items and pre- and post-meeting check-ins can also be conversation starters and good practices to use in your one-on-one interactions. I love that my grandchildren will ask, "What's on your agenda, Grandpa?" even in our weekly calls. The dialogue around meetings has become part of our family vocabulary.

What's on the Agenda?

Here is a sample agenda from one of my past Three-Generation Family Meetings:

- **Meeting Opening Ritual**
  Close computers
  Turn off cell phones

- **Tell a Story About . . .**

  Each person tells a story about their school, work, or what's on the top of their mind. Five minutes max per person.

- **Living Legacy Grant Reports (see Chapter 9)**

  My granddaughter Jessica reported on her safari trip, complete with a slideshow.

- **Noteworthy Updates**

  I reported about the new support group I had joined for people who had lost a spouse from cancer. (This agenda item allowed me to share that I had met a new lady friend there.)

- **Honors and Accolades**

  My grandson Benny shared an academic teaching assistant award he had recently received.

- **Roundtable**

  Everyone is invited to share anything else that they want the family to know. There are no rules here. For example, my grandson Aidan shared a dream he recently had. (I noticed his mom and dad, both psychiatrists, took notes.)

- **Post-Meeting Evaluation**

  Sometimes this is formal feedback on the overall

structure and content of the meeting. (The former General Director in me loves this!) Often this part is informal: I will ask people in conversation, or even in a follow-up phone call, what they got out of the meeting.

When speaking about Family Meetings in my work with grandparents, I'm often asked how to respond if anyone seems resistant to meetings. One way to make Family Meetings engaging for all is to invite everyone to submit agenda items.

For our family, the chairperson (initially Grandpa, but over time others have taken turns as leader) sends out a notice about a month ahead of time asking for agenda items to be sent to them two weeks before the meeting. Follow-up phone calls may be necessary for those family members who have not responded. Again, given my business background, I prefer this level of structure. Not everyone agrees, not even within my own family. However, that has never stopped me!

Even if my family makes fun, they like getting the agenda for the up-and-coming meeting beforehand. Formality is fine, but it shouldn't overrule enthusiasm. Last-minute agenda items, even once the meeting has started, are still welcome. My sending the agenda in advance serves to prime everyone to be prepared for the meeting.

Agendas can be built around some of the previously referenced items. Other ideas are:

- Each person tells a story of success or hardship since our last meeting.

- We each name something we are grateful for.

- Hold a timed discussion about a current event, social issue, or political goings-on in our country. (For example, the time my son Michael shared that he had joined the Socialist Party of Wisconsin.)

Keep in mind that not everything has to be serious or life changing. Family members planning a vacation might ask for ideas about places to tour if others have been where they are going.

Establishing Family Traditions

I read somewhere that all it took to create a family tradition was to do something three times. With that in mind, like the call to prayer in Jewish tradition or saying grace before a meal, I find it helpful to do some sort of repeated ritual that lets the family move from informally being together to transition into starting the Family Meeting. It might be reading a religious text or a favorite quote, or even ringing a special bell or sound that signifies it's time to get to business. A ritual to close the meeting is also helpful. We may do a big group hug (I'm a big fan of hugs) or gather in a circle for a big group blessing, each of us with our hand on the head of the person on either side. On that last one, that's where it's helpful to have a grandson who is a rabbi in the family. (Thanks, Ethan!)

You can even build traditions around creating the agenda. Here is a list of suggestions your family can incorporate to establish traditions.

- Tell a joke or a funny story that happened.

- Lead the family in their favorite song or sing a solo.

- Share a reflection about the family, the season, or the holiday.

- If you know a family member who had a great experience since the last meeting, ask in advance if they will share with the family what happened.

- If you know a family member who had a tough experience since the last family meeting, ask in advance if they will share with the family what happened.

- Do a big family hug before the meeting starts and after the meeting ends.

The agenda will change along with what's going on in family members' lives. There may be a different feel at different times of life, but that is the beauty and essence of knowing and growing in sync with one another.

When Family Meetings Get Serious

When life gets tough, having a strongly connected family unit becomes a gift beyond measure. Never was this more apparent than in the years during and after the final illness of my wife, Margaret, who passed away in August 2004. Family Meetings provided a forum for us to share painful thoughts and emotions that may have been too difficult to talk about had we not gotten some "practice" at being open and vulnerable around each other. Our enhanced communication wasn't only an emotional balm; it was an operational godsend. As a caregiver, I don't know what I would have done without my children's strong support, practical advice, and words of love from near and far. Our granddaughter Jessica moved from California for the summer to live with us and help us before returning to college. I will never forget her compassion.

I'm convinced that the loyalty and sensitivity everyone displayed during those grief-laden times were cultivated by the important discussions we'd launched in "normal" times. And thus it continues. Working toward mutual respect and understanding, and trust and forgiveness, is an ongoing process. Sometimes it's a joy and at other times it's a struggle. What Family Meetings do is to provide a forum for those important discussions.

Two years after Margaret's death, I began dating a wonderful woman who was my companion for over a decade. We met in a support group for bereaved spouses. I knew it might be strange for the rest of the family to think about me having a lady friend and that they might have some mixed feelings about it because of Margaret. My blossoming relationship became our meeting's agenda; we shared a heart-to-heart talk, a few laughs, and a few tears.

Talking about my relationship in this "public" setting also paved the way for conversations about peer pressure with the grandchildren. "What does it mean to be in a loving, respectful relationship?" easily led into a discussion of the #MeToo movement when the hashtag came to the forefront in 2017. What did my granddaughters experience at school? How were my grandsons standing up as allies? These were hard conversations, but we had a well-oiled practice in place to support them.

Here's what Family Meetings should never be: forums for hashing out vendettas or for calling anybody onto the carpet. Name calling, disrespect, or blaming are never acceptable. As my daughter, Ellen, observed:

Both my brother [Michael] and I have worked hard in Family Meetings to keep the focus on family strengths and on the strengths of each member. I've learned from management philosophy and from my background in family/human development that people are who they are. For me, the goal for our family is to celebrate and build on strengths. We don't operate on a deficit model—i.e., what's broken and what do we have to fix.

In other words, while conflict resolution is important for long-term harmony, the Family Meetings are not a place for that. That said, the anticipation of a Family Meeting might encourage family members to call or connect one-on-one beforehand if there has been tension. Reaching out after a meeting also does wonders for connection. For example, calling someone to thank them for sharing their vulnerability and offering help. I have often done that and received calls like that myself. A quick text saying, "Thank for your support," after a meeting is a simple yet positive touch of support between family members.

The Two-Generation Family Meeting

A friend's daughter, Yael, found great value in the larger extended Family Meetings, but also felt a need to better connect with her husband and two sons. Between work, business travel, school, and other activities, they often did not even have time to eat dinner together, let alone plan together.

Yael decided to try more frequent Family Meetings with her immediate family—those who live in the house together, as distinct from the Three-Generation Family Meetings.

Many of the items in this generally one-hour meeting are similar to a Three-Generation Meeting: having a special treat, time to catch up with each other, tell jokes, stories. Other items are specific to this smaller group: who needs help with homework, or what school activities are coming up this month. Given the busy schedules of families these days, some items may even be logistical, like who needs to be where, when, or finding out the soccer championship and the Science Olympiad are on the same day.

What's particularly nice about the Two-Generation Family Meetings is that children learn how to express caring and to give and accept help from one another. When one of Yael's sons said he did poorly on a test, his brother offered to help him study. Parents can coach their children in this more intimate group in a way that might disrupt the flow of the Three-Generation Family Meeting.

In the long run, Yael's family found that by doing monthly meetings with the smaller group, everyone was more receptive to the periodic extended Family Meetings. They got into the practice of setting time aside for open, trusted sharing. This may be something for you to suggest to your adult children to try at home.

Involving the In-Laws

Just the word *in-law* can elicit a variety of images and emotions and maybe a joke or two. I would love to see a world where everyone can be together and get along. I do, however, realize that in many marriages when a new couple comes together, they still refer to it as "my family" and "your family" when thinking of the grandparent generation. How wonderful if it could be "our family."

Elena, a former employee of mine, loved the idea of Three-Generation Family Meetings but wasn't sure how to approach the parents of her husband, Rich. Would they be receptive? Would they feel slighted if they weren't included? When Elena consulted me about this, I told her it is important that the offer be made so there is never a feeling of "Why weren't we invited?" It's so hard and hurtful when one set of grandparents feels like they are not as included as the other.

Elena spoke to her parents, who agreed that the meetings should be as inclusive as possible. Then she and Rich decided together that he would let his parents know about the upcoming meeting and invite them to attend. They held the meeting the day after Thanksgiving and gave the option of joining remotely to make it as easy as possible to participate.

How exciting it was when Elena called with a follow-up report. The two sets of grandparents have since forged an ongoing bond. Rather than a sense of competition, which can sometimes happen between grandparents, they see each other as allies around their shared love of their grandchildren.

The Power Behind the Meetings

If I ever doubt the power of Three-Generation Family Meetings, I remind myself of probably the most impactful agenda item, to me, of any Family Meeting we've ever had. Following our group discussion, we resolved to do everything in our power to ensure that no member of our family, regardless of financial resources, would ever lack for needed medical care or psychological support; that no young person would be prevented from attending college or trade school; and no elderly person would be forced to live out his or her days in isolation or poverty. One could draw a direct line from this resolution, made over ten years ago, to my living with my daughter and her husband in their home in Los Angeles today.

Your Turn: Journaling Expeditions

1. Plan a Three-Generation Family Meeting. Think about the next time your family will be together and send an invitation to set aside a time to talk. Invite everyone to share discussion items to create an agenda.

2. Create your own sample agenda to send to your family to prompt their participation. Draw from my family's sample agenda or come up with items that work for your family. Thought-starters may include a three-minute story of success since the last meeting, teaching Grandma and Grandpa to use the computer, planning for the next holiday, who needs help, etc.

CHAPTER 6

Plan to Connect (And How Technology Can Help)

Some grandparents lament the advent of technology as a barrier to their grandchildren: "They only pay attention to their phone!" On the other hand, technology can be an amazing gift, allowing families to stay connected with even more face-to-face time, albeit virtually, than in the "olden days." In fact, Avi and his grandpa Ira became closer after Avi moved halfway around the world, as he shares in this letter.

Grandpa Ira's (Virtual) Blessing

For the past six years I have been living and studying in Israel, thousands of miles from my family in the US. Even so, I can say without hesitation that I have never felt closer to my grandpa Ira (Bernstein), who is now ninety-eight. And for this I must thank a wonderful invention: videoconferencing.

I always had a very special connection with

Grandpa, but our bond was truly forged back when I was preparing for my bar mitzvah. He served as my tutor and devoted countless hours to training me in the Torah readings, Hebrew prayers, and synagogue rituals.

Fast forward a dozen years, and pretty much every Friday as the Jewish Sabbath approaches, I drop whatever I am doing in order to have a videoconference date with my grandfather. We talk for a significant amount of time, discussing the week that has passed, or stories from our family's history. Most importantly, I've come to truly value his wisdom and sage advice about whatever life challenges I share with him.

When it's time to say our goodbyes, Grandpa gives me the traditional "Blessing of the Children." I bend my head slightly forward and Grandpa raises his arms as if to lay his hands upon me while he chants the holy words—just like he would if I were there in person to receive this comforting blessing.

No exchange quite compares to seeing Grandpa's smiling face and "feeling" his hands on me. Knowing that these are among the most important years of my life, and among the final years of his, I feel unbelievably lucky to transcend the miles and to share this weekly ritual with my grandfather.

Avi Rosenbaum (24)
Stamford, Connecticut

A generation ago, chatting with children and grandchildren out of state meant being tethered to a corded telephone with costly, per-minute long-distance charges. To get face time in real time meant that somebody had to purchase an airline ticket and take time off from work. Multiply the expenditures of time and money significantly if you or your kids lived abroad.

Not anymore, thanks to free, easily downloadable internet-based telephone and videoconferencing systems like Skype, FaceTime, Zoom, WhatsApp, and more coming online every day. You may already be quite familiar with this technology; you may have even been a pioneer and "early adopter" when Skype first became available in 2003. Or maybe not. According to a 2012 report from the MetLife Mature Market Institute, only 12 percent of grandparents had embraced Skype as a way of staying in touch with grandchildren.[6] By 2018, 40 percent of grandparents felt they were technologically savvy, according to an AARP study.[7]

And it's safe to say that the vast majority of grandparents who use some form of technology to communicate are baby boomers (or even younger). No question: it's the boomers who are bridging the technology gap between their kids' generation—younger adults who grew up in a world of rapidly evolving digital communications—and their parents' generation—people my age who generally don't find these devices or operations terribly intuitive and can be intimidated by them. In fact, the same AARP study states that three out of four grandparents are on at least some type of social media platform. Six in ten (65 percent) are users of Facebook, outranking any other social media platform and at parity with the US adult population.[8] That may be the reason young people are leaving Facebook in droves ("Run! Old people are here!"), but it's still a good sign for grandparents.

---

6 "The New American Family: The MetLife Study of Family Structure and Financial Well-Being," MetLife, September 2012, https://www.soa.org/globalassets/assets/Files/Research/Projects/research-2012-metlife-family.pdf.

7 Brittne Nelson-Kakulla, "2018 Grandparents Today National Survey," AARP, 2019, https://www.aarp.org/content/dam/aarp/research/surveys_statistics/life-leisure/2019/aarp-grandparenting-study.doi.10.26419-2Fres.00289.001.pdf.

8 Ibid.

Technology Closes the Miles

Thanks to today's smartphones and tablets, you don't even have to be at home to videoconference, nor do you need to live especially far from your grandkids to find the technology useful. Hand-held media enables your grandkids to contact you at special moments—giving you a front-row seat at their spring concert or greeting you from the Eiffel Tower during their French club's school trip. They can see your expression when they tell you they were just accepted by their dream college. Should there come a day when you can't get around as well as you used to, having this technology in place will help the family look in on you.

The forementioned examples, however, are all instances of how technology serves as the vehicle for connecting, a device that simply enables you to link virtually with your grandchild. Beyond connection, how can you magnify your relationship using technology? If you're like me, you'll always think that being in person is better, and that it aches not to be together in person with grandchildren. We all know that's not always possible because of distance, health, or for other reasons. You can, however, make meaningful connections with grandchildren via technology, with the wide range of readily available platforms and resources that allow you to interact and engage in joint activities in real time.

Follow Your Grandchild's Lead in How to Communicate

Letting your grandchildren share with you their favorite platform for chatting is an excellent way to understand their technological world. How wonderful to know how they communicate with their friends! The key is to use the technology to do things together. Mail a box of ingredients ahead of time and bake something together onscreen. Share virtual tours together. I visited Israel, Poland, and the Art Institute of Chicago all in one morning, and all from my living room. Many not-for-profits arts and cultural institutions now offer private virtual tours with a small donation. My friend Barbara, a doting aunt, has set up tours of animal sanctuaries for her family. They do the tour together even though they join from four different states. She also follows other animal organizations on Instagram and YouTube just so she can share cute pictures and videos with her nieces and nephews. Schedule a watch party on your favorite livestreaming platform, such as Netflix or Hulu, and watch a movie together. Leave your phones on speaker so you can talk and react like you are together in a theater. Technology offers limitless opportunities to connect.

That said, don't be surprised or discouraged if your teenage grandchild who is never off their phone suddenly doesn't want to be on their device with you. Screen burnout is real. That's why it's so important to schedule time to connect. Kids are on screens all day for school, so talking to them after school may not be the best time if you want their full attention. Make sure they have been outside or have had a chance to decompress so they are ready to be with you. Allow your grandchildren to suggest how you will connect and let them teach you how to use the different devices or platforms. Adapt to their schedule but do ask to confirm a specific day and time for your next call.

You Don't Have to Be an Expert

As excited as I've become about Zoom, et al., I assure you I'm not about to launch into any detailed high-tech overviews. First, at the rate things are going, any cutting-edge trend I might spotlight on these pages could go the way of the eight-track tape or Myspace by the time you read this book. But that's not the only reason. I admit it: demographically speaking, I'm one of those *elder elders* for whom all this represents a brave new world I haven't fully mastered. Through talking to people and writing this book, I've started learning what some of the more tech-savvy seniors are up to, and I realize I've only scratched the surface.

Some years back, when I first started formulating my ideas for this book, I envisioned regular Family Meetings where everybody sat around the kitchen table writing in our notebooks about our common interests, undertaking discussions, and putting our conclusions on a whiteboard. I've had to face the fact that the nature of modern life—including, but not limited to, today's economic realities and COVID-19-induced restrictions on travel and social gatherings—would, all too often, preclude the in-person part.

So, while I still love nothing more than having all of my children and grandchildren under one roof, I've come to realize that communications technologies are making the world our kitchen table, rife with opportunities for sharing and embracing this as a part of our family culture. My family has wonderful interactions, for example, through exchanging group emails about personal, philosophical, or political matters. Emailing allows all the recipients to log on and respond at an hour that works within their time zones and busy schedules. It enables everyone to digest matters without confrontation or interruption, and to formulate thoughtful replies.

Here are a few thoughts about other modes of communication—ancient and modern—that we grand-parents can use to make the world our kitchen table. They don't offer the face-to-face pleasures of video chatting, and no technology can provide the psychological benefits for both grandparents *and* grandchildren of a walk on the beach or a real-life hug. But even in families that live only a town or two away from each other, those precious times may be few and far between, especially as the grandkids get older.

Find various paths to connect and go with what works. There's no "best" way of connecting with the younger generation. Creative, flexible grandparents know they must be guided by the situation. The trick is to weave back and forth between various modes of communicating, as situations warrant, and as befits different family members' needs at different junctures.

Go for whatever seems to work best for your family. Regular interactions build bridges between in-person visits where chasms might grow instead. Listed below are some ideas that worked in our family.

Social Networking

Social networking sites such as Facebook, Instagram, YouTube, and Snapchat—some of the ones popular around 2020—let you peek into your grandchild's world. Older adults are flocking to Facebook and other photo-sharing sites, so they need no introduction. If you are not yet connected, first ask yourself if it's right for you and if so, then ask your grandchildren to help you get set up. That's what I did. My granddaughter Kathryn set up a Facebook profile for me so I can view my family's posts, although I don't post myself.

But there are parameters to observe once you get

there. Social networking sites can offer a window into your grandchild's world. Open it but don't judge it. Resist the impulse to post anything or to comment on your grandchild's social media posts. Nor should you share their photos or status updates on your wall unless you have their permission. Don't initiate "friend" requests to their friends but embrace it (and take it as a big compliment) if some of them reach out to "friend" you! And never post pictures of your grandchildren without their permission.

Ask them where they are online and if they would mind connecting. Don't be offended if they decline. This is their space to interact with their friends. There are some video-sharing platforms, such as TikTok and YouTube, where you don't need permission to view their creativity. In fact, they can't tell you've watched their video unless you "like" it or leave a comment. You do, however, need to know their channel name to find them. Ask if they would mind sharing theirs with you.

You may not appreciate some of the language, photos, or declarations you see on your grandchildren's social media posts. We older adults, for the most part, have decidedly different definitions of appropriateness and privacy. So please do not be judgmental about what you see. That's a surefire way to be blocked from future access. That said, if you see something that raises a red flag about your grandchild's well-being or safety, advise their parents and look for help on how to handle it—offline.

And don't overlook the internet's other portals by which to connect. There are families that host their own webpages and reunion sites where grandparents can participate to their heart's content. But remember: if you regret posting something too personal, it may have already been reposted, shared, and stored by others online by the time you delete it. When in doubt, keep it off the internet.

Phone Calls

Personally, I'm big on the old-fashioned telephone call. I love hearing people's voices as a window into how they're feeling. I'm also a big proponent of just letting my grandchildren know I've had a hard day and asking them for what I call "a phone hug" or offering one to them. Either by voice or video, it's much more likely that you'll talk to your grandchildren if you schedule a regular time. If it turns out they're too busy, don't be reproachful or give them a guilt trip; be happy they lead such active lives! Nobody likes to talk to Grandma or Grandpa out of obligation, and no grandparent should want to be talked to simply as a chore ordered by parents.

Oh, and don't bother leaving a voicemail if you miss

them. Apparently, for the majority of young people today, it's out of vogue to listen to voicemail. Although I understand if you can't help yourself! So if you do leave a message, don't take it personally if they admit to not listening to it.

Be flexible. If the frequency is too much or the times consistently don't work, readdress the schedule. For years, my grandson Ethan and I used to enjoy a phone call on Friday afternoons. Now that Ethan is a rabbi, Fridays are a busy time for him to wrap up his personal and professional activities before the Jewish Sabbath begins at sundown. We moved our chats—some of them quite brief, others not—to a different day when they can be a pleasure, not an intrusion.

Text Messaging

If you don't text message, you're missing out on what's become the leading way that today's young people like to connect. Like it or not—and I can't say I do—text messaging has vastly outstripped phone conversations as a way to keep in touch with the young.

If you need to get hold of a grandchild quickly, texting offers the best chance of success. Even if they don't have a block of time to return a phone call, they will almost always respond immediately to a text. It's not my first choice to connect, and I'm going to keep championing the old-fashioned phone call as best I can. But texting is here to stay and it's definitely effective. As learners, we need to come to grips with it.

I have one friend who texts his grandson every morning just to say "I love you." His grandson texts back, "I love you too, Grandpa." It's a quick exchange, but let's both know someone is thinking about them. During the COVID-19 pandemic, many families set up a group text to be able to stay connected. Another friend, Grandma Bobbie, asked her grandson to help her set up the group chat on her phone—adding names and numbers to the contact list so she would know who was who. You wouldn't know by her messages that it takes her a while to peck out each letter and carefully select the perfect emojis. And sometimes she has thought of leaving the group when the dings and vibrations get overwhelming in a fast-paced conversation. "Don't do it," her daughter urged.

If the above scenario sounds familiar, I have the same advice for you. You don't want to be left out of a single opportunity to connect with your family. This is their world. You may not understand everything about it. It's likely not the way you would do it. You don't even have to read every text in a long conversation. But you are in, baby. Never give that up.

Email

Let your grandchildren know if email is still more comfortable for you. Ask your grandchild for help to set up an email address just for you even if they have moved onto other social platforms. I often email my grandchildren my thoughts about something we've talked about or links to articles that I think they'll enjoy. When the grandkids are traveling outside of the country, email is terrific. No more waiting forever for a postcard, though they are still nice to get. Or remember those crinkled aerograms?

Here's a best practice: text them to let them know you've sent them an email so they will look for it. While email is great for us, it's not part of a teen's daily communication repertoire. It may sound redundant on your part to text someone to tell them you've sent them an email, but that is you accommodating their communication style because you love them and want to connect. That's what grandparents do.

The "Ancient Art" of Letter Writing

I've never been much for letter writing, to be honest, but I do recognize that a handwritten note from a grandparent may become a treasured keepsake. It's also a nice thing to occasionally cut out a newspaper article that you think a grandchild will be interested in and send it in the mail. And who doesn't love a surprise package! It could be something you packed or baked yourself. With easy online ordering and often free shipping, why not send a "thinking of you" gift just for the sake of it. I think it's nice for younger generations to experience how we used to define social networking: going to the mailbox and finding a real letter among the bills and circulars from a real person who loves you. Do they reciprocate? Rarely via snail mail, but they'll show their appreciation in a future phone call, email, or text. One day they may find a treasure trove in the form of your letters and be thrilled to have what are now valuable keepsakes.

Meet Them Where They Are

Does anyone need further proof that creating strong ties with grandchildren is a gift that keeps on giving for generations to come, for generations we may never see? Whether or not we received that gift ourselves, we can still give it. It's about saying yes to trying and going the proverbial extra mile to meet our grandchildren where and how they live and for them to do the same for us, whether they are across the street, across the country, or across the globe.

If you've resisted jumping on the communications-technologies bandwagon for whatever reason, I urge you to consider the importance of *trying*. If you're embarrassed or worried about a learning curve, don't let that stand in your way. I'm in pretty much the same boat. At this point, whenever I require any sort of tech support, I call on the best teachers I know: my kids and grandkids. If no one's available, I'll get a student from our local high school or middle school to come over and tackle my problem or try and talk me through it for a relatively modest fee. I've promised myself to make time to enroll in a computer course geared for seniors. A wide array of such courses is available in adult education programs and at community centers in practically every city and town in America. None are very costly, and you can even find some—mostly through seniors organizations—that are free of charge.

Although computers have become much more affordable throughout the years, not everyone has the means to purchase one or to pay for an internet connection. In that case, your best resource is your local public library where you can log on for free. If you need help setting up a free email address, the staff can help. And then you'll be just a few keystrokes away from connecting with your grandchildren wherever they may be studying, living, working, or traveling.

Letters from Grandchildren:
What I Learned from My Grandparent

In the letters below, these grandchildren tell of special

memories of their grandparents, courtesy of technology-assisted communication.

An Electronic Treasure Trove

As I look back on moments that defined my relationship with Gramps, I recall his seventieth birthday celebration when his children and grandchildren gave him a gift that changed the way he communicated. We gave him a subscription to Prodigy, one of the early internet service providers. He embraced the new technology and became one of the few of his generation to become internet proficient.

And now, through the wonders of Gmail, I have a collection of more than five hundred emails from Gramps.

I have reread many of Gramps's emails over the past few days, and I am reminded of what a wonderful example he set for his grandchildren.

On tzedakah, the Jewish tradition of charity: "You will be pleased to learn that your brother and I will deliver food packages for Rosh Hashanah at the end of the month. He will do the driving and shlepping while I do the navigating. This is a landmark date 'cause I started doing this job with your aunt when she was five or six." (8/10/2010)

On devotion to his spouse: "Today is truly a day to remember—a landmark anniversary for us! Just think, fifty-eight years of being together. I was a bashful twenty-six at the time. Gram was a ravishing twenty-two. A real beauty. We were sure it was the real thing." (9/8/2006)

I am eternally grateful to have had a role-model like Gramps, and I am extremely lucky that he left me an electronic treasure trove of memories, advice, and Gramps-isms. I'll always remember the lessons he taught me, and my Friday evening inbox will never be the same.

Jeremy K. (30)
Chicago, Illinois

Opapa Online

My Opapa Larry loved his iMac computer and relished being an octogenarian in a wired world. He started his day by logging on to his favorite news sites and ended it with late-night games of online Solitaire and poker. In between, he stayed in touch with friends and family around the globe via email, often forwarding us the semi-appropriate jokes that he and his buddies circulated.

I'll always remember our hilarious webcam sessions while I was in college. My floor-mates would crowd around my monitor and shout, "What's new, Opapa?"—that was his trademark greeting: "SO VAHT'S NEW?"—while laughing uproariously at those semi-appropriate jokes. It was hard to have much of a conversation because his hearing was pretty awful, but just by looking at him, grinning, in an old white V-neck undershirt, you could tell that he loved the attention from all the cute girls.

If he'd lived a little longer, I'm positive he would have joined Facebook and had a ball with it—updating constantly, posting political articles and silly cartoons, "liking" every post and friending everyone he met. Young people often don't appreciate being indiscriminately friended by older folks. But Opapa was such a character, I doubt anybody would have minded.

I don't even want to think about the stuff he might have tweeted.

Arielle O.S. (24)
Wilton, Connecticut

Your Turn: Journaling Expeditions

1. Write about a memorable experience to share with your grandchildren that will give them a picture of what it was like to be young in a world without cell phones, personal computers, or the internet.

2. Make some notes on what your own hopes and wishes are regarding when and how often you will get together, call, or video chat with your grand-children. Find out what works for your family members and set a schedule together.

3. Keep an ongoing wish list of technology skills you'd like to master, products you'd like to own, or services you're interested in trying. Ask one of your grandchildren to teach you.

CHAPTER 7

Navigate Interdependence with Your Adult Children

L et's face it: life-cycle changes are humbling. Whether it's the physical transformations of aging or even happy changes such as becoming a grandparent, they force us to face certain realities that we may not be ready for. After all these years at the helm, we've gotten very accustomed to our leadership role as the Adults in Charge. Oh sure, we've been practicing the fine art of "letting go" from the first time we put our kids on a school bus. Still, it's tough. Because *nothing* can change the fact that for as long as we live, we will always be their parents, and they will always be our children.

Even with all the years of evolution and adjustments in our parent-child relationships, the arrival of a grandchild signals a new era. The circle of life has turned, and now there are two sets of parents in the room: them and us. The profound delight we have as we gaze upon this new being also carries with it some fear and loss we're not used to thinking about or expressing. Suddenly we feel old, no longer in charge, and there are so many unknowns. *Will I be a good parent?* you may

wonder. *Where do I fit now?* may be troubling your mind.
And there's nothing like feeling insecure to make one
defensive. Then, just when we hit a groove and think
we have it all figured out, the grandchildren become
teenagers. Family dynamics change all over again, not
only for us, but especially for our adult children. There's
nothing like a teenager to make a parent question their
parenting.

Paradoxically, becoming at ease with mutual interdependence can help family members build up their
individual strengths, competencies, and self-reliance.
When others have stepped up to the plate for you, you'll
want to become a person who is able and willing to step
up to the plate for others, if it's possible. So, why are we
so afraid of interdependence?

What Is Interdependence?

There's no question that human beings possess an
innate hunger for independent action, individuality,
and self-determination. US culture especially embraces
the cruciality of acquiring the skills and the confidence
to live successfully on one's own. And we dutifully
transmit those values to our children and grandchildren.
I don't think there's a single reader of this book who I
would have to sell on the importance of cultivating one's
personal independence. Let's take that as a given, shall
we? But the ability to depend on others when necessary—

especially our families—for physical, emotional, and economic support is no less important to our survival than being able to do it alone. Nor is it less noble. We need the skills, the courage, and the good sense to know how to do both at the appropriate junctures.

I became more aware of this issue in 2010 when I took an adult education course at Northwestern University titled "Families in the 21st Century." My fellow students were, for the most part, the baby boomer parents of young-adult offspring. I observed an interesting phenomenon. During our classroom discussions, nobody had a problem intellectually embracing "collectivism" as a powerful, twenty-first-century *political* value. We all agreed that nations could benefit immensely from sharing resources and developing joint initiatives in such critical areas as global economic development and climate research.

But when it came to *personal* values and family living, an altogether different paradigm prevailed. Independence and autonomy were prized above all else, and the flip side, immediately labeled as "dependence," elicited shudders all around. As it happened, a number of these parents at the time were experiencing the phenomenon of "boomerang kids" following the 2008 economic downturn. These parents were distraught that their empty nests had recently been refilled by twenty-somethings who were unemployed or underemployed and behaving like spoiled teens—borrowing the car without refilling the gas tank, having friends over who pillaged the refrigerator and liquor cabinet, and leaving around their messes and dirty laundry.

Wasn't it possible that the regressive, inappropriate behavior my classmates were observing may have been rooted in their kids' anxiety about the economic hand that America's so-called millennials had been dealt? Maybe it could help everybody in the family to talk more about their own fears, embarrassment, and expectations.

"Well, I want them out of the house!" one father responded firmly to my comments. "Independent is the thing to be." Most of the others nodded vociferously in agreement. Even the professor didn't dispute the notion that lacking a firm grip on the brass ring of independence—a proud, all-American virtue if ever there was one—clearly represented some sort of failure, weakness, or sin.

Why We Struggle with Interdependence

Many people associate being dependent on someone else as a loss or deficit, especially when there is financial support involved. Our adult children may struggle with feeling they have something to prove, thinking that being an adult means no longer needing help from "Mommy and Daddy." For us grandparents, we just truly want to help if we can. Dependence can also mean a loss. As we grandparents age, we are alternately concerned about being a burden, or losing our independence when adult children start having opinions on where and how we live (especially if we live alone). However, when adult children and their parents practice interdependence and rely on each other, all three generations become closer.

What often happens in too many families is that the fear of being dependent on another family member wins. Parents and adult children institute a knee-jerk, misguided "Declaration of Independence" because they believe that's what's supposed to happen now. Don't share what's troubling you. Don't ask for what you need. *Don't tell Mom!* This leads to mutual frustration and guardedness, futile attempts at mind reading, personal implosions, and interpersonal explosions—events that breed miscommunication and distance at precisely the times that frankness and durable connections are needed most.

In our pull-yourself-up-by-your-bootstraps culture, we have become so deeply wary of being, becoming, or appearing *dependent* that we often overlook—even stigmatize—interdependence, which is one of our most gloriously human and important family values.

Is It So Wrong to Accept Help?

Fast forward ten years from that day in class at Northwestern, and I find myself living with my daughter and her husband in LA. Concerns about social isolation during the early stages of the 2020 COVID-19 pandemic had them urging me to move from my condo in Deerfield, Illinois. Grandparents moved in with their adult children and grandchildren to help while parents worked from home and managed remote learning for the kids. In other cases, entire families—the adult children, grandchildren, even the dog, moved back in with parents to create safe "pods" to shelter-at-home together. That raised its own set of questions: Is Grandma, who has been an empty nester for years, expected to cook and clean for all as the matriarch of the house? Who disciplines the children now that multiple generations are living under the same roof?

What I told my classmates then was still true in 2022: First, I validated their frustration but pointed out what I thought was obvious: that setting basic ground rules and coming up with some creative alternatives could transform shared living during challenging times due to the economy or COVID-19 into a win-win situation. Grown children could contribute by setting up technology networks, cleaning out the garage, and shredding old documents, for example. Household chores should be divided so that the burdens would be less on everyone. Developing imaginative menus might become an enjoyable shared activity. I wasn't blind to the challenges of having adult kids and their families boomerang back home. Nor could I ignore the tarnished pride and sheer difficulty for a grandparent to acknowledge they needed help from their children without feeling like a burden. But truthfully, it didn't sound so terrible to be able to go for an occasional after-dinner walk with an offspring I'd never expected to be under the same roof with again. And all the in-between times with grandchildren that I never expected seemed glorious.

With multigenerational living, no matter what prompted it, grandparents are gifted time with children and grandchildren. We also get a chance to see our adult children in action as parents. That creates a whole new narrative of how we see and understand them. My colleague's daughter, Rachel, didn't know how much she would appreciate that until her mother observed and complimented her parenting. When it's just a phone call once a week, you can't see it. Now, all living together, Rachel told her mother that she felt like her mom finally witnessed her as an accomplished adult and parent. And she said that allowed her to relax and better accept her mother's offers to help. She no longer perceived these overtures as being judgmental.

And Then Life Happens Again

It seemed that as soon as we adjusted to a new routine devised in response to the pandemic, there was a vaccine.

While it did not end the COVID-19 virus once and for all, it did beg another set of decisions as schools reopened and people were allowed more mobility again. In some cases, families moved back home. In others, they came to embrace multigenerational living.

For me, I'm glad I'm with family. Yet, I still did not sell my home for another eighteen months. It took more than a year to accept that this wasn't temporary. In my defense, many did think the COVID-19 pandemic would be short-lived. But even after the vaccine was available, new variants emerged. At ninety-two, I still feared losing my independence and becoming completely dependent on my children. However, living with them gave me a firsthand view of the very real anxiety they had about me living alone. Now that I understood it from their perspective, I could see that staying with them permanently was the right thing to do. But selling my condo was emotional. I lived there for twenty-five years, eight of them caring for Margaret until she succumbed to cancer. I knew I was gaining a new and deeper relationship with my adult children, but I mourned the loss of my independence.

We Are More Connected than We Admit

In many cultures, of course, interdependence is woven into the fabric of family life. This is apparent among immigrant families—for practical reasons and historical ones—as well as others in our midst who cling to highly traditional, cultural, ethnic, or religious values. It is normative in many cultures outside the US for extended families to live nearby or under one roof. In the US, however, standards and expectations of family life are more aligned with an exalted American dream that prizes individual attainments and comfort above communal obligation.

As much as they resist it, however, parents and grandparents are more connected than they may admit. According to an AARP survey in 2018, 81 percent of grandparents say they play an important role in their grandchildren's lives. Of those, 38 percent are babysitters and daycare providers. Grandparents spend an average of $2,562 annually on their grandchildren, totaling $179 billion per year. The highest category of spending was for the 21 percent of grandparents who contribute to their grandchild's school or college tuition, spending an average of $4,075 annually.[9]

The study also found that 11 percent of grandparents live in the same household as their grandchild. While I don't recommend you share this out loud with your adult children, especially in the heat of an argument, but 77 percent of grandparents thought that "parents today are too lax with their children." Seventy-nine percent thought child discipline was worse today than it was in

---

9 Nelson-Kakulla, "2018 Grandparents Today National Survey."

their day.[10] I thought you would want to know this in the spirit of "You're not crazy." But for the harmony of interdependence and intergenerational living, I suggest you keep that to yourself.

Pooling resources by moving in together after un-employment, lost stock-market gains, dwindling pen-sions, and housing foreclosures has its win-win aspects too. The biggest winners are the grandchildren who have yet one more person to love them in their lives.

Let's Talk About It

I think it's truer now, more than ever these days, that families must make an active commitment to discuss important issues openly and respectfully. Otherwise, they may find themselves in a most unpleasant predicament: struggling fiercely to maintain some semblance of independence or succumbing to interdependence that is filled with nonstop conflict. That's a situation that could really spiral into the kind of unbalanced *dependence* that most families want to avoid.

If you fear you may be headed in that direction, the first thing to do is to take a deep breath. Acknowledging our changed reality—that we've all entered a new stage of life—and talking about it, is a first step to defusing the fears that accompany it. This does not happen all at

---

10 Ibid.

once. Patience, compassion, humor, and the belief that we are not diminished by interdependent relationships will keep us strong and secure as individuals and as a nurturing family unit. (See Chapter 8 for specific techniques to approach difficult conversations.)

Boundaries: Navigating a Permanent Place in Your Grandchildren's Lives

At the core of the dance of interdependence is a healthy understanding of boundaries: What is the role of parents? What is the role of grandparents? During times when you are dependent on each other and all the times in between, clearly defined boundaries lay a strong foundation on which interdependence can be built.

Here's an important boundary, and one your adult children will appreciate your respecting: You are not your grandchild's parent. Nor are you your adult child's full-fledged partner in raising the next generation (except in circumstances in which grandparents share or obtain custody of their grandchildren). Transitioning from being the parent to being the grandparent is a new ball game, with new rules and new roles.

Mouth Shut, Wallet Open

Gilbert, a grandparent who spoke with me after one of my many speaking engagements, said sometimes he felt "mouth shut, wallet open" was the only way to maintain full access to his grandchildren. He and his wife, Alice, had a standing Thursday night date with their grandson practically from the day he was born. While Grandpa Gil loved the time with his grandson, he felt it was more transactional for his daughter, as she only seemed to engage with him during pick-up and drop-off when she needed something. Grandma Alice, however, saw it differently. She kept a saying by her bed that said: "Dear Lord, please help me to remember to take the time to bestow the kisses today that I want loved ones to remember tomorrow." Indeed, after twenty years of Thursday night dinners plus hundreds of adventures, museums, root beer floats, and more, their grandson now drives himself over to his grandparents' house and picks up dinner on the way.

Negotiating time together with grandchildren can be a struggle between parents and grandparents. But never forget the true loving relationship at the center. It's the grandchild who benefits when the parents and grandparents don't let their own defensiveness or this-is-the-way-it-has-to-be stance get in the way.

"Mouth shut, wallet open" does contain some basic truths about human relations. *Nobody* appreciates tactless, relentlessly opinionated purveyors of unsolicited advice. And *everybody* appreciates people who are, to the best of their abilities, genuinely and joyfully generous, both materially and spiritually. In that sense, we should all go through life guarding our tongues and opening our "wallets" and hearts to support one another!

Generational Trust: Should You Keep Secrets?

There's an adage that says grandparents and grandchildren are so close because they have a common enemy: the parents. A better version of this could be that grandparents and their adult children are so close because they have a common love: the grandchildren. No matter how grandparents and their adult children feel about each other, both want to ensure the younger generation is safe. That includes hoping and praying that if your grandchildren are in trouble, they will always have someone—you included—with whom they can talk.

As grandparents, we want our grandchildren to feel they can confide in us, but trust must pass through all generations. At times, I have taken the approach of "not keeping secrets from parents, no matter what," when I didn't want to jeopardize the trust in my relationship with my adult child.

This matter was raised at several of my speaking engagements. Grandparents would say, "But I treasure my special bond with my grandchild," or, "But my grandchild feels comfortable talking to me," or, "But what if the kid really needs to talk to someone they can trust?" Especially during the teenage years, where the peer group is most often where a child gets their ideas or shares their innermost secrets and concerns, I sensed a gray area—that grandparents wanted to be there if a child needed help.

So, what do you do when a grandchild asks you to keep a secret from their parents? The right person to whom to address this question is the parents. I asked the parents of my six grandchildren what they thought. "If your child asked me not to tell you something, what do you want me to say?" We could lay the ground rules that are acceptable to them in advance.

"We have raised our children to be honest and moral people, and we can't imagine them doing anything that would merit such secrecy," said my daughter-in-law, a psychiatrist.

I hesitated for a few seconds, then said, "Shall I help you remember some things your husband did as a teenager?" We all giggled.

"We trust your judgment," my daughter-in-law continued. "If it's a tattoo on her butt, I guess I don't need to know. But if she's suicidal, taking drugs, drinking alcohol, or doing anything that might harm her, we need to know right away."

These conversations with my adult children changed my former position on "no secrets" to allow for a little wiggle room. Now I say to my grandchild that I will listen to what they have to say, but if they are drinking, using drugs, pregnant, responsible for getting someone else pregnant, asking me for money for an abortion, or otherwise causing any danger to their own health and safety or that of other people, I will talk to their parents. But a step in between there would be to ask my grandchild, "Why don't you feel comfortable discussing these or any other matter with your mom or dad?" I will help my grandchild think through how he or she would talk about this with their parents, but within a clear time frame that we can agree on.

When is the right time to have a conversation like this with your grandchildren's parents? The sooner the better. The important thing is to talk to the parents and set the parameters. Having the talk about underage drinking, STDs, or other things that may come with growing up is never going to be easy, but nevertheless, it's important to have this talk. "*My* child would never do that," they might say.

"Guess what, they might, so just indulge me," I answer.

This conversation with adult children can help to create an environment where people feel comfortable sharing and trusting, and where there is communication across the generations of family members. This is important both in terms of what grandchildren are telling grandparents, as well as when or if your adult child wants you to share stories from their childhood— because grandkids may ask. Know which stories are okay and which ones are off limits. For example, maybe your child almost died from alcohol poisoning at a party when he was sixteen. As a parent, he might say to you, "I may or may not tell my kids what happened when I was sixteen, but I'd like to be the one to do it when the time is right." The person who actually experienced the situation and lived to tell the tale is the one to tell their own child, or anyone else in the family, if they so choose. It is not your story to share.

It's Okay to Say No

Part of healthy interdependence and clearly defined boundaries is for family members to understand that they have a right—even an obligation—to say no to requests for help that they cannot handle, and to do so lovingly before burnout occurs or resentment festers. This is a delicate balance that can teeter over to unhealthy enabling or excessive dependence unless there is clear, open communication.

Generally speaking, adult children need to place the needs of their partners, their children, and their employment first. And grandparents should not compromise their own financial security, physical or emotional health, or marital harmony by overextending themselves for adult children or grandchildren.

My own family's interdependence was certainly put to the test on a number of occasions. There were periods during which family members became unemployed, and Margaret and I helped financially to pay several mortgage payments, buying a used car, and making sure the grandkids could stay in school or have childcare. When Margaret became ill, we were the ones who had to ask for help. I spent eight years as a caregiver, and there were situations in which I felt I needed additional support from my children and grandchildren. Twice-a-year Family Meetings became our forums for discussing the new normal that now prevailed in our lives, and each of these meetings sparked conversations that would continue and evolve in the intervening months. We all had to learn to ask for what we needed, and our family is so much stronger because of it.

And we may still make mistakes. Particularly in living together, boundaries are blurred at times. I'm working on that every day. It's a part of the normalcy of life when a family stays deeply connected and allows each other to grow as individuals.

Letters from Grandparents and Grandchildren: What We Learned from Each Other

In the spirit of interdependence, this first letter is from a grandparent about what she learned from her adult daughter.

A Russian Adoption

The enormity of what we had done didn't hit me until we were saying our goodbyes at Dulles International Airport in DC. My husband, Bob, and I had just returned with our daughter, Toby, from three weeks in Russia where she had completed a foreign adoption. Igor Sergeivitch Kaleznik, age just-turned-two, was now hers. And ours.

"Please," I asked one more time, "let Dad and I come home with you for a few days."

"No," she replied. "I have to bond with him on my own."

"So you bond, I'll do the laundry."

"No," she said with the familiar determined set to her lips that I knew so well. "I have to do this by myself."

So, we hugged and kissed, and Toby, a single parent, put Igor into his stroller and left for her own apartment. We got into the security line for the flight back to Chicago. I cried.

It wasn't going to be easy. Igor had spent all of his two years at Orphanage No. 4 (of forty) in Rostov, Russia, where the director told us, "You must always say 'no' to him. We raise our children to be tough because it's a tough world out there and they must be tough to cope with it."

And tough they were. On the orphanage playground, where the ages ranged from eighteen months to four years, the children bit and scratched each other over toys and turns on the seesaw. They fought over where to sit and where to stand. Generally, the caregivers let the children work things out themselves— even the littlest ones just starting to walk had to learn to defend themselves.

Almost nine months later, Igor (now Nathaniel Benjamin and called Nate) is a darling and delightful child. He is in nursery school two mornings a week and plays well with others. He loves the park and playground. He no longer throws food onto the floor or items into the toilet. He speaks English now and can say "I'm mad!" instead of biting or hitting.

How did all this come about? Through months and months of patience and endless loving care from our daughter. Through limitless hours of playing, singing, and dancing with him. Through infinite readings of books and playing in the sink with water toys. Through time spent with therapists, social workers, and nursery school directors. Through months and weeks and days spent devoted to Nate.

He is the love of her life. As most mothers, she knew she would love her child, but never realized how absolutely crazy she would be about him. Friends keep saying what a lucky little boy he is to have found a loving family. No, we are the lucky ones. To Bob and me, he is a gift, a blessing, a special child. To Toby, he is everything and the soul that completes her life.

Esther L. Manewith (77)
Chicago, Illinois

This next letter affirms the special place that grandparents hold in a grandchild's life.

Hearing a Grandmother's Voice

A few years ago, when I was a teenager, I fell in love with a boy who just really wasn't right for me in any way. He was rude to my friends, but when they urged me to leave him, I didn't listen. My mom saw the way he treated me, which wasn't very good, and kept questioning why I was still with him. Her disapproval worried me deep down, but I ignored it.

Then, one day, my grandmother called me and said: "Baby, what's going on with you these days? I hear that things aren't good." I knew, that moment, it was over with my boyfriend. After her phone call, I broke off all contact with him and felt more secure in my decision than I ever thought possible.

Whenever my grandparents step into a situation involving my siblings or me, I know it must be serious and I should take notice. Let's face it: it's not the same as when a parent steps in. Parents will nag you about everything and anything, but grandparents just get to be sweet to you! I know that if they are genuinely concerned about me, they must know what's best and I should listen carefully to what they have to say.

Z.H. (22)
New York, New York

Your Turn: Journaling Expeditions

1. Write about a time when you were dependent on another person. How did it make you feel about yourself? What did you learn from the experience?

2. Recall a time that someone relied on you. Write about how it made you feel.

3. Has a grandchild ever asked you to keep a secret from their parents? How did you respond? What were the consequences of how you responded?

4. Have a conversation with your adult children about secrets. What, if any, secrets are okay for you to have with your grandchildren? Write down everyone's reactions to the conversation and the parameters that you set together.

5. Write about a time when you disagreed with a parenting decision your grandchild's parents made. How did you respond? Did you stay silent? Speak up? What did you learn from the experience?

CHAPTER 8

Practice Forgiveness

By the time we reach the grandparenting stage, we've all endured some of life's unforeseeable twists and turns: tragedy, disappointment, loss. And then along comes this brand-new bud on the family tree. Even the most disaffected soul can feel the unabashed stirrings of a poet: a new leaf, a new dawn, purity, innocence, sweetness, and light.

"A baby is nature's way of giving the world another chance." It's an uplifting quote everyone has heard or felt themselves in one form or another. And never is it truer than when that baby is your own grandchild. Grandparenting can provide a renewed sense of wonder and purpose for us as older adults, as well as a rekindling of memories. Memories of our own children's early years—inhaling the scent of a newborn, pushing a little one "higher, higher!" on a swing, taking them to their first movie. Even memories of our own childhoods, and our own parents and grandparents, so long ago.

But then the bucolic record comes to a screeching halt and is replaced by the recollection of the sulking disrespect from your own children when they hit high school. You didn't understand why they shut you out as they became adults. You can recall their accusations: "You were always too hard on me!" or "You just don't understand!" or "You were never there for me!" Your grandchildren becoming teenagers and watching them interact with their parents may reopen some of those old wounds for both you and your adult children. While possibly painful, this is also a gift. It was likely the arguments during those years—when teens were pushing the limits and yearning for their independence—that set the patterns that simmer today.

When there's old baggage and festering resentment with our adult children, it will take more than shared delight over grandchildren to wipe away years of contentiousness or resentment, or to reopen lines of communication that have long been clogged. In certain aspects, grandparenting presents an opportunity to be a more engaged, impactful, loving family member than you may have been capable of being three decades ago. But it's not a parenting do-over that wipes your slate clean. No matter how noble our intentions, our grandchildren are just that: our grandchildren. And our adult children—our grandchildren's parents—are ultimately the gatekeepers. You must conscientiously ask for and practice forgiveness, including from yourself, to make amends with the generation in between.

Overcoming Past Conflicts

I realized that the first thing I needed to do was examine my interactions with my adult children. This was no small hurdle. There was an abundance of love between us, but there were unresolved issues too. When we disagreed on something, or simply felt tired and short-tempered, our default mode was a hopelessly outdated one. It harkened back to the days when my children were the combative kids and I was their authoritarian dad. We needed to shed this baggage if we were to effectively nurture and guide the *next* generation, and to serve as worthy examples for them.

That requires us to take an honest look at the past and figure out how it might stand in the way of fulfilling family relationships in the present and future and then try to do something about it.

The good news is that grandchildren at every stage, be they newborns, teenagers, or beyond, open windows of opportunity for doing that healing work. After all, you and your adult offspring have something extraordinary in common: you're both parents. Presumably, they're flooded with overwhelming awe and love for the life they've been called upon to nurture and protect, as well as tremendous uncertainty and worry about whether they'll be equal to the task. Welcome to our world, kids! Because isn't that just how we felt—and continue to feel—through every stage of parenting and with each highly idiosyncratic offspring?

When They Realize We Did the Best We Could

No question, there's truth to that insufferable mantra that's passed from generation to generation: "Someday when *you* have kids, you'll understand!" What will they understand? That for the most part we did the absolute best we knew how under our circumstances at the time.

Some offspring seem to get this *without* having to struggle through parenthood themselves. But for those who needed an extra jolt, the recognition of their own parents' humanity and best intentions can be so humbling that it unleashes a rush of warmth and gratitude. It may hit them as soon as their first baby is born. Sometimes it doesn't hit them until their children are teenagers—as they sit up and wait, worried beyond measure for a child who's an hour past curfew. "If they're okay, they are in so much trouble!" Followed by, "I can only imagine all the times I must have terrified my parents back then." This is not the time for an "I told you so." Rather, jump on that sentiment and cultivate it with care, and all three generations will reap the benefits.

Acknowledge Past Hurts

The reality is that some of the stumbling blocks in our

relationships with our adult children may be products of a past that is impossible to undo (or to redo). For example, if you underwent an acrimonious divorce, or you were a workaholic when your children insisted they needed you most. You may have been obligated to give your attention elsewhere—to an ill parent, to a child with special needs, to an organization or business that rested heavily on your shoulders—but the end result was that your absence made a particular child feel undervalued.

The unhappy memories and recriminations can go both ways, particularly if your children's teen years and early twenties were laden with conflict. The times you felt scared to death because they were acting out in ways that put them in harm's way; the times you felt wounded when they seemed to flout your most deeply held values. And their resentment over your missteps—in coming down too hard on them . . . or not hard enough.

Even if it's all old baggage that's barely relevant anymore, and the details have become hazy, you and your adult children may still feel weighed down by it.

Overcoming Ongoing Conflicts

Past demons are bad enough. *Ongoing* conflicts, fed by a wellspring of anger that keeps replenishing itself, can be even more destructive. You may harbor a cauldron of resentments about their choice of life partner, their work, their religious or political attitudes, sexual behavior, where they live, their friends, and so on. They may have their own simmering stew dedicated to your opposition and perceived judgments, your laundry list of old mistakes or behaviors they are less than fond of.

Like leftovers of a past that cannot be undone, this doesn't bode well for an unfettered grandparenting relationship with the "innocent bystander" who is your grandchild. In fact, sharply differing notions about raising children can provide you and your adult children with a whole new universe of issues upon which to disagree. This can add bitterness to the brew and exacerbate things even more by the time your grandchildren enter their teenage years.

Forgiveness Is a Priority

If you're already living this way, you know how exhausting it can be and how corrosive it is to relationships, body, and soul. Will you take the first step and accept that you have a chance to courageously lead your family forward onto a better path?

I believe that we as grandparents must plow fertile ground for the process of healing by establishing a practice of forgiveness in our families. This means acknowledging past hurts and missteps, rebuilding trust, and seeking and offering forgiveness. And this includes not only with our adult offspring, but with their spouses or significant others, with the in-laws (the "other" grandparents), with ex-spouses who may be parents of our grandchildren, and with the grandchildren themselves once they are old enough to grasp the concept.

What does it mean to promote a practice of forgiveness?

- **Don't ignore signs** that we may have hurt a family member. If we have, reach out to them with concern and humility.

- **Don't mask our own hurt feelings** with aloof or angry behavior that is difficult for others to decipher and address.

- **Strive to make compassion our default mode** in how we view and interpret a family member's actions.

- **Use respectful language** and a loving tone of voice when we talk about what is bothering us.

- **Acknowledge that being open to forgiveness—** seeking it, offering it, promoting it—**is a core value in our family.**

Forgiveness Starts with You

If it feels like I'm saying the responsibility is on you to initiate these conversations of forgiveness, I am. You are the only one who can control your own behavior, and changing your behavior automatically changes the dynamic of your interactions with others. Then there's that amazing grandchild! You have so much to lose by waiting for someone else to start a conversation when you can start it today with reflection and planning. Don't wait for the other person to go first no matter how wronged you feel.

Forgiveness and reconciliation are core values of all the world's major religions and are central attributes upheld by many nonbelievers as well. For many years, I've embraced the Jewish tradition of phoning my family members, friends, and colleagues (of all backgrounds) around the fall High Holy Days to wish everyone a good year ahead, and to ask their forgiveness for anything I may have done to wrong them, especially if it was unintentionally. You certainly don't have to be Jewish or religious to undertake an annual commemoration of forgiveness! Examining your family's beliefs and expectations regarding forgiveness, and sharing stories that emphasize its value, can serve as an excellent agenda item for a Family Meeting.

Forgiveness is a process that may take an exceedingly long time. But it, too, starts with a single step. Often that step is a candid conversation with a loved one in which you say sincerely: "I'd like to talk about [an issue from the past], because I don't want it to get in the way of our family's wonderful connection and feelings about the future."

The unfortunate paradox I've observed through decades of assisting families in crisis is this: a reluctance to speak candidly (but carefully) about areas of potential conflict is the very thing that *ensures* that eruptions of anger and hurt *will* occur, and it makes the resultant discord that much harder to resolve. Learning to discuss the tough stuff when times are good is what helps families build a foundation of trust, intimacy, and mutual understanding that can withstand life's storms.

Acknowledge the "Separate Realities"

Let's face it: there are separate realities for parents and children in practically every family. Your adult child remembers being slighted or hurt in one way or another. You have a completely different memory, or even none at all, of that incident. Saying, "I don't remember, but I'm sure I didn't mean to hurt you," not only doesn't help, but it may be incendiary. *How can you not remember that?* your adult child may think. Even relatively minor, long-past separate realities have the power to destroy relationships when people don't acknowledge them and make amends.

San Francisco-based psychologist Joshua Coleman, the author of *When Parents Hurt: Compassionate Strategies*

When You and Your Grown Child Don't Get Along, affirms this idea:

> Honor the "separate realities" nature of family life. Just because you made decisions with your child's best interest in mind, doesn't mean that they were experienced in the way that you intended. Don't try to prove them wrong . . . Take responsibility for whatever mistakes you have made as a parent. If there's a kernel of truth to your child's complaint, speak to the kernel of truth.[11]

If your adult child shares an experience that involved you, even if you don't remember it, don't deny that it happened. If someone feels something, it is real for them. The immediate response should always be empathy and acknowledging that the feelings are real. Some responses from you might be expressing what your intent was if you do recall the situation. Or you may want to acknowledge the hurt and ask for more time to think about it. No matter how you respond, you can learn so much from honoring the idea of separate realities. Look at reopening the past as a way to more deeply know and connect with your adult child.

---

11 Joshua Coleman, "Growing Pains," *Greater Good Magazine* (blog), July 8, 2010, https://greatergood.berkeley.edu/article/item/growing_pains.

Forgiveness Letters

Married authors and counselors Joyce Vissel, RN, and Barry Vissel, MD, are staunch advocates of writing letters to seek forgiveness to loved ones you believe you have wronged. They describe a forgiveness letter as "one of the most powerful healing techniques we have ever come across."[12] Even if the letter is never sent (and it shouldn't always be), for the writer it represents "an inner process of resolve and completion through taking responsibility and becoming vulnerable."[13] And for a potential recipient, say the Vissels, a letter of forgiveness can be better than a phone call or a face-to-face meeting because it is "the least invasive or confrontive method. It doesn't put pressure on the recipient to respond or react in the moment. It allows time for reflection."[14]

Here are the Vissels' guidelines for crafting your own letter of forgiveness. You'll notice some overlap with my Tender Loving Communication (TLC) conversation questions that follow.

- Take responsibility for your part, how you hurt the other person, rather than give any attention to

---

12 Joyce Vissell and Barry Vissell, "A Powerful Forgiveness Technique," The Shared Heart Foundation, July 2000, https://shared-heart.org/a-powerful-forgiveness-technique/.

13 Ibid.

14 Ibid.

how they hurt you. In fact, if you haven't expressed your own hurt, this may need to be the first letter. However, for healing to be complete, you eventually need to take full responsibility for your own actions, or even thoughts.

- Be vulnerable. Reveal your own sadness or remorse for causing them pain.

- Let them know you are not asking them to respond in any way. You are doing this for yourself, not to be forgiven by them. If they write back, it needs to clearly be their own choice.

- If you can, include some appreciation for this person. Look at who they are rather than the painful interaction with you.

- Write the letter with the choice of not sending it. Asking for forgiveness is, after all, a very personal and inner process.

- Share the letter with someone you trust and get their feedback.

- If it feels right, send the letter.[15]

Do you need to write yourself a forgiveness letter? Holding on to resentment against yourself can be just as

---

15 Ibid.

toxic as holding on to resentment against someone else. Poor behavior or mistakes don't make you a bad person. Don't hold onto past shame or regret over things long past. Accept the fact that you—like everyone else—aren't perfect. Accept yourself despite your faults. Admit your mistakes. And, perhaps, write yourself a forgiveness letter.

TLC: Tender Loving Communication

With past grievances hopefully resolved, there are always plenty of interactions to inspire new conflict. You ask where your grandchild has applied to college. Your adult child interprets it as you saying they are not on top of their child's future. They share that they got a call from their child's teacher, and you start offering solutions to try to fix it when they never asked for help. What's a grandparent to do? Try a little Tender Loving Communication, or TLC.

Fruitful discussions enabled by TLC are far better predictors of intergenerational harmony and thriving connection than grim mandates like "mouth shut, wallet open." There is much more for you, your children, and your grandchildren to look forward to when you have clear expectations, open hearts, and a conscious commitment to keep trying—and keep talking—as your lives and circumstances change throughout the years.

Of course, for most of us there's an unmistakable

learning curve before we master TLC. It's an ongoing process that requires significantly more discipline and forethought than "Just Say Everything" if that's been your default mode throughout life. And it requires greater discernment and courage than simply resigning yourself to "Just Say Nothing."

TLC means asking ourselves some honest questions and giving ourselves some honest answers as we approach important conversations with our adult children and, as we and they grow, with our grandchildren. When we are talking about people we love, they're all important conversations! At the same time, a number-one concern voiced by grandparents I've worked with is: *How do I know when it's appropriate to speak up about my concerns or opinions to my adult children, and when it isn't?*

Here are ten questions to help you decide whether it's advisable to bring up a topic—using TLC, of course—or whether you're better off biting your tongue after all. They can be helpful in determining if, when, or how to voice a concern or initiate a conversation, be it about past grievances or new worries. These questions can be useful as a gauge to mitigate future rifts.

Am I teaching something of value by saying it, or is it better left unsaid?

For starters, it may help to look to the words of twentieth-century theologian Reinhold Niebuhr (which were slightly adapted to become the iconic Serenity Prayer used by twelve-step programs). One does not need to be a person of faith to embrace its wisdom:

> God, grant me the serenity to accept the things I cannot change. Courage to change the things I can. And wisdom to know the difference.

Be honest with yourself in asking: What is my purpose in making this statement? Are you speaking up to promote a family member's welfare (and it's perfectly legitimate if it's your own), to correct a genuine misunderstanding or right a true wrong? Or are you following an impulse to open an old wound or to prove, once again, that you were indeed right?

Being unmuzzled does not give a parent or grandparent license to "bite." For example, if your loved one has experienced a crushing disappointment, telling them "I told you so," (or its equivalent) does nobody any good.

When should I say it?

In general, it is better to *not* delve into hot-button issues during times of high emotion. Wait until things have calmed down. In years past, when my children were bringing up their children, they would sometimes phone me to offload a litany of parenting concerns. Very rarely did they ask for my opinion; they simply wanted to let off steam. I often felt I had useful advice for them— some insights that might help based on my professional knowledge and my years of parenting *them*. But all those years of experience has taught me something else too: highly agitated individuals are seldom receptive to unasked-for prescriptions for how to fix things. They're much more likely to shoot the messenger.

How do I know if I should say anything at all?

You'll know because you'll ask. To this day, if my children or older grandchildren share a vexing problem with me, I will calmly say a version of the following:

- "Would you like me to tell you what I think?"
- "Should I choose a better time?"
- "Should I say anything at all?"

Then I abide by their answer without challenging it. If it is clear that the problem is persisting, I'll bring it up at a time that is less emotionally charged and ask again if they want to hear my ideas. It is important that they know I respect them as competent, independent adults. This is key to all of us being able to embrace our alternating roles as teachers and learners.

How do I say it?

Tactfully. This isn't a tall order if we always make a

conscious effort to address each other with gentleness and kindness. It never ceases to amaze me that we seem to speak more graciously and respectfully with complete strangers than we do with our own families! Charitable, compassionate speech begins at home. Caustic language, sarcastic subtexts, and accusatory assumptions have no place in our discourse. If the walls of your home really did "have ears" and could talk, what would they say about the way you speak to each other?

Should I say it in private?

Family Meetings can be a good forum to bring up topics that are difficult to discuss. Some family members can inspire others with the courage to speak frankly. But in certain instances, privacy may be more appropriate. When in doubt, ask. The more comfortable you become with asking instead of assuming, the fewer missteps you will make.

Must I say it in person?

There's a school of thought that important issues should always be raised face to face, and certainly there are situations in which it would be cowardly or insensitive to do otherwise. Oftentimes, a sympathetic look, a big hug, or a gentle smile will greatly reduce a listener's antagonism. That said, difficult conversations shouldn't be put off indefinitely. Videoconferencing may offer an alternative to in-person, in the case of prolonged absence, insurmountable distance, or health concerns that prevent gathering together.

If I can't interact in person, is it better to say it over the phone, or email, or by text?

I have observed that family members sometimes find it easier to delve into uncomfortable topics via telephone. There are times that expressing ideas in a carefully crafted letter or email will enable you to present them without interruption and give your child or grandchild time to process before responding. That said, putting delicate matters in writing can come back to haunt you; plus, they can also be forwarded to parties with whom you had no intention of sharing your personal business. Weigh your words very carefully before you hit the "send" button.

I would never be one to initiate a serious conversation by text, but you may have family members who swear by texting. In fact, it may be the only way to get a response from them. Beware of taking easy offense in a text exchange. It's so hard to convey feelings in such short bursts of communication. "This sounds important, when can you talk by phone?" may be the right text response to avoid misinterpretation.

If I inadvertently cause pain by what I do or say, how do I take responsibility and learn from it?

It's inevitable: we who try will occasionally fail. Even the most loving families fall prey to missteps and misunderstandings. The trick is in how these painful events are handled. A family whose members actively endorse a practice of forgiveness will make mutual understanding its highest priority—they will not tolerate grudges, excessive blaming or shaming, or protracted periods of estrangement. However, taking a little breather after a serious disagreement can help all parties to cool down and gain perspective. If your actions cause ill will, regardless of how well intentioned they were, apologize immediately and make sure you ask what was hurtful about your actions so that you understand (without making assumptions) why this occurred.

You need to be open to the fact that perhaps there is a pattern in your behavior or speech that you need to address. It's possible that you may have struck a nerve that has nothing to do with you, and in responding to your questions about what went wrong, your adult child or grandchild may recognize some issues they would do well to address. Each of us owns our own individual, intensely personal, and idiosyncratic history of our family. If we don't try to share those histories, we will forever remain mysteries to each other.

If I'm the one stung or confused by my children's or grandchildren's words or actions, am I able to model positive behavior by candidly sharing what I'm feeling?

Grandma and Grandpa can have hurt feelings too. One would hope that at our stage in life we are above pettiness in our interpersonal relations. At the same time, we are not robots or doormats. Recently, I felt slighted when I tried reaching my grandson several times over the course of a week and he did not return any of my calls. When he finally did call, he explained apologetically that he had been busy traveling and coordinating an academic conference. Now it was my opportunity to teach about forgiveness. I candidly shared my hurt feelings while at the same time reflecting on the fact that I should have been more patient and understanding, and not have taken his slow response so personally. Honest conversations about adverse emotions or interactions can be opportunities for enhanced closeness—they need not simply be swept under the rug.

How do we fully resolve conflict if it does arise?

Conflict is an inevitable part of being a family and of being human. Episodic conflict will not destroy a strong family. This brings us (again) full circle to the family's culture of forgiveness. But there's more to it than that. Harmonious families triumph over conflict by giving it a double whammy. Its members are both slow to anger and quick to forgive. These attributes, which are cornerstones of all the world's religions, are among the most valuable ones for us as family elders to model through our own behavior and interactions.

Don't we all know people who go through life being quick to anger and slow to forgive? These unhappy souls are primed to swoop down upon and magnify every perceived slight and believe the worst of everyone. Instead of striving to be consensus-builders and peace-seekers, they appear driven to divide, conquer, and control. They corner you with tedious, bitter rants about being perpetually wronged: victimized by ungrateful family members, mean-spirited employers, and incompetent service people.

Older adults who fixate on how others treat them and have little concern about how they treat others will inevitably isolate themselves. On the other hand, it's hard for even the most curmudgeonly family member to stay mad at a grandparent with a generally upbeat disposition, a generous heart, and a ready sense of humor.

If you and your family can resist pouring your collective energies into the black hole of acrimony and recrimination, you've won half the battle toward being the best, strongest, most mutually supportive, and loving family there is.

One other word of advice: be patient. Relationships

don't become tense overnight, and the tensions don't defuse overnight, either. In the best-case scenario, your adult child will echo your sincere wish for a flourishing relationship and will eagerly look to you as a hands-on grandparent. Or you may need to reach out repeatedly for a while. Don't give up. With an open heart, remind yourself that there's no greater joy than watching your grandchildren blossom and no greater satisfaction than helping them along.

Your Turn: Journaling Expeditions

1. Identify two to three issues that would benefit from a Tender Loving Communication (TLC) approach.

   This exercise challenges you to examine some of the issues you've considered raising with your adult offspring, and to practice sharing them using Tender Loving Communication. *Note: this exercise can be adapted for dialogues between grandparents and (older) grandchildren, in-laws, spouses, siblings, etc.*

   To get you started, here are two sample dialogue openers, presented through two different lenses (one to let off steam, and one to actually use):

   a. **Bite Your Tongue**, which demonstrates how we sound when we speak carelessly without TLC—

i.e., making statements that could easily wound feelings and spark conflict.

b. **TLC**, which conveys the emotional truth of what's on our minds and speaks to others' hearts.

Sample Issue #1:

- **Bite Your Tongue:** "Son, do you know how long it's been since you made the time to go anywhere with me? I see you are busy again. Sorry I'm so boring to be around."

- **TLC**: "Son, every once in a while, when it's convnient for you, I'd love the opportunity for some alone time with you to talk about adult topics like the family and politics."

Sample Issue #2:

- **Bite Your Tongue:** "Your mother's been gone almost five years now—may she rest in peace—and I must've asked fifty times for somebody to come and help me clean out that attic space where she kept her sewing materials. I know everybody's busy, but I have to start thinking of myself, maybe selling the house. What the heck's gonna become of me if I can't get anybody to give me a few lousy hours to deal with her stuff?"

- **TLC**: "Kids, I want us to feel comfortable discussing

what may lie ahead for me as I grow old. I'd like to be able to talk to you about my concerns about aging, disability, and quality-of-life and end-of-life issues—and I want to hear your thoughts too. I don't plan on going anywhere soon, but it would be a big load off my mind to start putting some thoughts on paper about all this, and wrapping up some loose ends in the house."

Your TLC Dialogue

Now craft your own dialogue opener. If you are feeling that way, write down a Bite Your Tongue version to get it off your chest. Then craft a TLC version that you could use to begin a dialogue.

To download a copy of this practice sheet, visit https://www.grandparentsunleashed.com/worlds-meet-resources/

Conversation #1 is with _____ about

_____

Bite Your Tongue Version:

TLC Version:

Conversation #2 is with _____ **about**

_____

Bite Your Tongue Version:

TLC Version:

Conversation #3 is with _____ **about**

_____

Bite Your Tongue Version:

TLC Version:

2. As a parent, what do you think you're ready to forgive yourself for? Write yourself a forgiveness letter.

CHAPTER 9

Create a Legacy Now

In the many years that I've been listening to grandparents share their hopes and dreams, their regrets and fears, the word *legacy* is one that comes up over and over. It's a word that carries much weight and many meanings. Most of us, of course, are concerned about our legacy in its most tangible manifestation: a financial inheritance or endowment.

Regardless of our financial bracket, we grandparents hope to maximize whatever we may be able to pass down to our heirs. We want to make an investment in our grandchildren's lives that goes beyond money. I'm sure I didn't coin this phrase, but it captures the idea beautifully: We want to leave *values*, not only *valuables*.

In this chapter, I provide two initiatives: The Four Jars, and the Witkovsky Family Living Legacy Foundation. Both offer concrete ways that you can follow to bequeath both values and valuables while you're still around to enjoy it. I say, "Don't die until you're dead." Why not create a living legacy by working with your grandchildren while you're still alive?

Grandson Ari shares how his "Gaggie" did just that, in his letter honoring what he learned from her.

Playing the Market with Gaggie

Not every teenager has an octogenarian investment guru whom he telephones daily and refers to as "Gaggie." But thanks to my grandmother, Rita Butensky, I've fallen in love with playing the stock market like I used to play Fantasy Football.

It all started several years ago when Gaggie bought ten shares of Disney for my two brothers and me. After seeing how profitable it was, I eagerly began purchasing some stocks on my own: Apple, Google, and Verizon. (Being a triplet, I often do things in threes.) Now, the minute I get home from school, I rush to my computer to see how my stocks are doing, and then I call Gaggie to discuss the market. She always has the same cautionary message: "Great job, Ari, but remember . . . I was lucky."

Gaggie started investing at a time when the economy was much more robust, hitting it big with AT&T before it split into the Baby Bells.

She constantly exhorts me to buy a stock only after learning everything I can about the company, to follow all my stocks closely, and to proceed cautiously in this volatile global market.

Whenever the red arrow of doom appears on my screen, I break into a sweat over my decreasing portfolio. And then I call Gaggie. Her comforting words and common-sense wisdom remind me that you can't always win, and that in the stock market, just like in life, sometimes you just must accept a loss and move on.

Ari Scheinthal (19)
Cherry Hill, New Jersey

We all hope that the deepest guiding principles of our own lives will be carried forth by our grandchildren as they forge their unique paths into the future. Will they proudly transmit our cultural heritage? Will they treasure our Bubbi's handwritten recipe book from the old country? Will they teach their children to love the Chicago Cubs? The reality when it comes to values—as we saw in Chapter 4—is that there is no guarantee that our grandchildren will embrace the values that we cherish.

We can only hope that our grandchildren will appreciate our traditions and beliefs and understand why they matter to us so deeply. We can do our best to instill those values through ongoing proactive, conscientious sharing throughout our lifetime, and by the example of how we've lived each day. Even if our grandchildren don't share all of our values, or even agree with them, they will respect them and know they are important to us. With our example, we can trust that they will grow into people of strong morals, passions, family-feeling, and conviction—the kinds of people who will strive to leave behind their own enduring and meaningful legacies.

Naturally, in thinking about our legacy to our grandchildren, we must never ignore the powerful influence of the generation in between—our adult children—and the fact that the beliefs and values they wish to instill in their offspring rightfully take precedence over ours. Adult children sometimes take paths that strongly diverge from how we raised them. It is terribly important never to undermine or criticize their way of life through our words or our actions. I don't underestimate how difficult such situations can be—for example, religious differences—when one generation is more devout or less observant than another—or divergent political convictions.

Yet, in most faiths and belief systems, the desire for

"peace in the family, harmony in the home" is a core aspiration. As family elders, we need to steadfastly uphold this principle, as it may be the most important legacy we can leave.

For my family, I created two initiatives: the Four Jars Project, and the Witkovsky Family Living Legacy Foundation. The Four Jars prompted one-on-one conversations about values between me and each grandchild individually. The Witkovsky Family Living Legacy Foundation invited the grandchildren, all the siblings and cousins, to share their values and experiences collectively. It also aimed to keep them connected to each other, to encourage lasting bonds.

Before inaugurating these two initiatives, I carefully reviewed them with my daughter Ellen and son Michael and their spouses to get their input and make sure they were on board. If, for whatever reason, they were not in favor of it, I wanted to respect the primacy of *their* wishes for *their* children. Plus, I wanted to assure them that they were under no obligation to contribute to or take over the funding at any juncture, unless, of course, they wanted to.

I also wanted to assure them that this was not in any way a commentary about them, their parenting, or their ability to provide for their children. This was about my relationship with my grandchildren and my desire to enrich the whole family, and to do what I could while

I was still around to connect and learn and grow from experiences along with them. With that understanding and their blessing, I forged ahead.

The Four Jars Project

The Four Jars is a concept I don't claim to have originated, but here's how it works in my family. I purchased four mason jars and gave each one its own label: Helping, Spending, Saving, and Investing. I gave a set of jars to each grandchild on their thirteenth birthday, along with a modest amount of money. I continued to send a small amount of money each month for one year after that.

It is the concepts the jars teach that is most important. They are:

1. **Helping:** Live a life of charity and kindness.

2. **Spending:** You are responsible for your own happiness, so take risks.

3. **Saving:** Live life with a sense of vision. (And the value of delayed satisfaction for something bigger.)

4. **Investment:** Money that grandparents or other family members have set aside for college, which teaches accepting love and help from others.

I've spoken to other grandparents who have launched the program with $20 in the form of four $5 bills, and they continue to send four $5 bills each month for a year. I've seen others do it with four $1 bills, or even loose change. The amount of money is not what is important. Grandparents may send the jars and not include money at all. What's most significant is the conversation this initiative prompts with grandchildren around the concepts that each jar represents.

If you find yourself hoping your grandkids might distribute the money equally among the four jars, think again. While the grandparents may decide how much money to give, only the grandchild can decide how to divvy up the money to put into each jar.

Even middle-schoolers are old enough to start learning to make smart choices about their money and to take pride in financial "independence." That's another reason why I instituted the program of the Four Jars.

Your grandchildren's allowances from their parents, their birthday or holiday gifts, and earnings from odd jobs (such as lawn work, babysitting, or shoveling snow around the neighborhood) are apportioned within the four jars that stand alongside each other, kept in a spot of their choosing. It may likely be in the children's bedrooms—the one space in the house that is private to them. Wherever they keep the jars, the idea is that no one else can see them and pass judgment or second-guess their decisions. The savings eventually make their way into the children's bank accounts. They can decide on worthy charities that they'd like to contribute to with the money they put into the charity jar. This is another reason why it's good for your adult children—their parents—to be on board. Parents can offer a trip to the bank or to help on the technical side of making a donation when the children are ready.

When my granddaughter Merete was in middle school, she told me she wanted to put all her money into the Spending jar, but she suspected that wasn't right. I told her it was her decision. Even as a budding teenager, she was learning the balance with money we do all our lives. During a family outing about that time, I was tickled to see Merete buy herself a delicate ring as a souvenir, taking obvious pride in the fact that she had paid for it out of her Spending jar. Similarly, each week she was expected to bring a dollar to Hebrew school to contribute to charity. Instead of asking her parents for the cash, she always made sure she had it in hand before she got into the car after taking it from her Helping jar. These lessons have stayed with her, even now that she is in college.

In my family, the Investment jar is not money given to the child but rather money invested on their behalf that they could access for college or other educational purposes. That said, when my grandson Benny wanted to learn more about investing and what it meant, with his parents' permission he took advantage of my offer to meet and talk to my broker. His kind heart spilled over into this area when he realized he could make investment decisions based on a company's values, telling the broker, "I do not want my money invested in any company that makes war or weapons."

In the well-known words of the Chinese philosopher Lao Tzu: "Give a person a fish and you feed them for a day. Teach a person to fish and you feed them for a lifetime." My hope is that the education of the Four Jars will inculcate habits and ideals that will carry on long after my grandchildren have left those childhood bedrooms.

The Living Legacy Foundation

During my many heartfelt discussions with grandparents about their legacies—financial and otherwise—something kept nagging at me. Almost all those discussions began with somebody declaring solemnly, "After I die . . ." as the preamble to their ideas. This was the case whether the grandparent was fifty-five or eight-five, rich or poor, or anywhere between. I asked myself: "Why do we have to be dead before the fruits of our labor can be put to good use? Why can't we savor the outcomes and experiences along with our heirs?"

As it happens, *I'm* the "relic" who conceived of what

my family considers one of the most exciting shared activities we've ever undertaken: the Witkovsky Family Living Legacy Foundation. Like many of you, I was eager to help underwrite some of my grandkids' dream projects, educational pursuits, and travels. Plus, I wanted to be around to see their ventures bear fruit.

And that was what sparked the idea. It's been such a rewarding undertaking for our family that I'm laying out the nuts and bolts with you as a guide should you wish to create a Living Legacy suited to your family's distinctive relationships, needs, goals, and means. It's an original concept I'm thrilled to share.

What is the Living Legacy Foundation?

In our family, the Living Legacy Foundation is essentially Grandma and Grandpa funding projects submitted by our grandchildren to a Board of Directors that is made up only of the grandchildren—all siblings and cousins— for approval. We decided that our grandchildren could participate once they had reached their thirteenth birthday. It is a system we set up to fund the dreams and ambitions of our grandchildren in a way that lets siblings and cousins connect, stay close, and care about one another's interests, passions, and struggles.

The process of an application form forced my grandchildren to think through more deeply what they wanted and why, and we hoped it would encourage long-term planning skills in general. Calling it a "Board of Directors" elevated the importance of each grandchild's role and empowered the grandchildren to take responsibility together. The formal process also helped to set expectations for the grandchildren, and it allowed us to be upfront and transparent about our intentions with their parents.

To be clear, the Living Legacy Foundation is not a legal entity making charitable grants. While the foundation may teach some of the skills of philanthropy—namely writing proposals, creating budgets, and presenting follow-up reports, all of which is required for anyone submitting an application—the main purpose is to keep the next generation of siblings and cousins connected and invested in each other's lives.

How much does it cost?

Let me point out that you do not need to be a Granddaddy or Grandmomma Warbucks to get a Living Legacy Foundation off the ground. Even a relatively modest fund of several hundred dollars total per year can provide a meaningful and extremely satisfying experience for all. How much money is available each year is determined by the grandparents in advance. Grandchildren tailor their requests accordingly (to your set budget or their own conscience).

I did not need extensive rules about this in my family other than the requests had to be related to education or career. Thankfully, that loose guideline and a sense of responsibility from among the grandchildren was enough. In fact, I've never received more than one project request in a year and have only funded four projects since I initiated this. The grandchildren know this is special. Since you set the rules before the first project is even funded, give some thought to a need for any ground rules. Do you want to set a limit to how much can be requested in a single application? Is there a cap to the total amount available each year for all grants combined? Can someone receive more than one grant in a year or in consecutive years? We did not need this in our family, but you know your family dynamics and your own finances best.

We have two adult children and six grandchildren— so there are six Board members in our family. In scenarios with many grandchildren, you will want to be very clear about your overall financial commitment with the potential for so many requests. You may also want to engage your grandchildren's parents or other sets of grandparents to aid in the funding of projects. Involving another set of grandparents can make it easier, as there will be more people contributing to a pool of money. There may be some projects that parents themselves prefer to fund.

What does the Living Legacy Foundation fund?

Your grandchild identifies an activity—a travel experience, a course or enrichment program, or a purchase of equipment, materials, etc.—that relates to their education, their career, one of their major interests, passions, or goals, or an avenue they are very curious to explore further.

Through a formal process that grandparents and adult children prescribe, cousins and siblings form a Board of Directors (no adults allowed). Only Board members can submit requests, and anyone on the Board can do so. Submitting a request does not automatically guarantee approval. For one, grandparents will likely want to establish a cap to overall spending, which means not every request will get funded. Note that per our family's guidelines, requests must be education- or career-oriented. That was my stipulation. So, for example, a trip to Aruba just for fun would not qualify for funding.

Once a request is approved by the Board, it goes to grandparents for funding. Grandparents are not allowed to veto a request that has been approved by the Board. That was another of our family's rules, but you can choose whether or not this is a fit for your family.

Project requests in our family have been for study abroad programs, computers to launch a new business, and funding for job-search coaching. The Board doesn't automatically approve funding for every project that comes before it. They ask questions about the viability of projects and the sustainable impact. As the grandparents, ours is the easy and rewarding part, making their projects possible and then watching everyone share in each other's excitement over their achievements.

Who is on the Board of Directors?

In short, your grandchildren. In our family, we decided that thirteen is the proper age for children to join the foundation's Board of Directors with full voting rights. My son created a lovely certificate to present to each new Board member in commemoration of this expanded role, which was signed by every Board member.

Is there a Chairperson of the Board? I don't know because the adults do not sit on the Board, not even Grandma or Grandpa. In fact, we are not allowed in the room, be it physical space at a family gathering or virtual space via teleconference. Other than the giggles I hear through the door, the conversations are the purview of the siblings and cousins. And that is by design.

For families with only one grandchild, you will want to think whether this is the right process for you. The good news is the formal application helps grandchildren better research and plan, and with the post-project reporting requirement, the whole family learns what your grandchild has learned. In this case, the application process still has merit, although the approval will fall to the grandparent.

How does the Board of Directors make decisions?

Any of the grandchildren can initiate a project by submitting a short, simple request form to the Board. The request should provide a brief overview of the proposed project including why it's important to them, what the associated costs are for the project, what percentage they are asking the Foundation to underwrite, as well as how they plan to cover the remainder (if applicable). The request may be made in the form of an informal email, or by filling out and scanning the Living Legacy Foundation Request Form. Here is a sample of the form we use in our family. (Visit https://www.grandparentsunleashed. com/worlds-meet-resources/for a downloadable version of this application form.)

Witkovsky Living Legacy Foundation
Request Form

Submitted by:	
Date:	
Preferred Email:	
Preferred Phone Number:	

Proposed Project / Activity / Purchase (P/A/P)

Project Description:	
Related links (website, etc.):	
Why do you want to undertake this P/A/P?	
How will this P/A/P further your education or career?	
How do you believe you and/or others will benefit from your P/A/P?	
Explain how equipment, product, or activity helps your work, enriches your life, brings you closer to your goals, or helps you identify your passions.	
What is the time frame for the P/A/P?	
By when do you need the funding for the P/A/P?	

Budget

Amount requested from the Living Legacy Foundation:	$
Total budget for project:	$
If the request is only for partial funding, how will you cover the rest?	

Itemize key expenses associated with the P/A/P (if applicable)

Item	Amount	Funded by
	$	
	$	
	$	
	$	
Total Cost	$	

Plan for Follow-Up

What sort of teaching and learning experience will you provide the family with afterwards (i.e., share travel journal or photos; a formal report on a course or conference at a future Family Meeting, etc.)

Additional Comments

Board Decision

The Living Legacy Foundation's Contribution	$
How/when shall the money be transmitted?	
If the request was denied, or if the dollar amount was less or more than requested, what was the reason?	
Board members' comments/ suggestions, if any. (This can be an attached email thread.)	

The proposals are reviewed by the Board and voted on via email or by phone, unless the timing coincides with a holiday or family celebration and the Board can get together in person. In that case, the Board convenes behind closed doors until they reach a unanimous decision as to the funding recommendation they will pass on to the grandparent: to fund the proposal, to fund it partially, or not to at all. And how I love hearing the muffled sounds of laughter and lively debate wafting through the house when Board meetings are underway! This says to me that creative ideas are being shared, relationships are being cemented, and responsible approaches to finances are being inculcated.

Once the grandparent receives the approved request, they write a check to the grandchild for the specified amount. It is the responsibility of the grandchild to implement their project as it was outlined.

A Program of Learning for the Whole Family

Each Living Legacy Foundation recipient is expected to report back on their project be it through a travel journal or photos, a PowerPoint presentation at the next Family Meeting, a video, or whichever way they can, to create a learning opportunity for the rest of the family.

This idea of inviting grandchildren to present about experiences that are transformational to them is a wonderful practice for your family, whether these experiences were funded by a Living Legacy Foundation grant or not. It can further fuel the life passions of your grandchildren and inspire desire for additional learning from every member of the family.

Our Family's Living Legacy Projects

The Witkovsky Family Living Legacy Foundation con-
tributed toward my grandson Ethan's tuition when the
scholarship funds at his rabbinical school were suddenly
cut. It paid for my grandson Benny to journey to the
US-Mexico border as part of a course he was taking on
immigrants' rights at Vassar. My granddaughter Kathryn
was funded for a GMAT review course when she was
interested in pursuing an MBA degree to enhance her
career in the corporate world.

One grant went to my firstborn grandchild, Jessica, for
an extraordinary eight-week trip to South Africa. Jessica,
a wild-animal trainer and manager, covered half the cost
from her own savings and the Foundation underwrote the
rest. When the family got together for the next Passover
holiday—and my eighty-fifth birthday celebration—
Jessica narrated a fascinating slideshow of her journey. I
was taken aback by the beauty of her photography of
the creatures in the wild and the African terrain and sun-
sets.

Even more gratifying to me was the excitement in
her voice and the delight in her eyes as she regaled
us with tales of the animals she had observed in their
natural habitats, the interesting people she met, and
the unfamiliar new culture she had embraced. It was
hard to believe that this confident, very competent
young woman had been identified with some learning

disabilities as a young child. Through early intervention and hard work, she succeeded in overcoming those early deficits by identifying her life's passion and forging her unique path.

Jessica's slideshow elicited much enthusiasm and many interesting questions from the rest of the family. It was sharing at its best. Through Jessica's trained eye, I was thrilled to see a part of the world that I will likely never visit and overjoyed to be part of the "village" that helped her to get there.

A Program that Grows Up with the Grandchildren

My granddaughter Kathryn moved to Chicago in February 2015 to follow her boyfriend who had been transferred with his work. She left a successful position in partnership marketing with MGM resorts in Las Vegas to make the move. After six months in Chicago, however, she was getting nervous about her job prospects. She called to let me know about a career coaching program at Jewish Vocational Services (JVS) in Chicago. She thought it was a good program but could not afford the fees while she was unemployed.

I suggested to Kathryn that she apply for a Living Legacy Foundation Grant, and so she did. Without the Family Meeting again until Thanksgiving, she filled out the application and sent it to her siblings and cousins by email. The request was supported unanimously. It also gave Kathryn something else that she needed: empathy. It turned out that one of her cousins had also gone through a period of unemployment after graduating from college, and he was able to give her advice and commiserate.

Keep an Eye on the Valuables

In evaluating our legacy, it is also crucial to take a cold, hard look at the "valuables" part of the equation. The reality is, even when everyone has the best intentions, clashes over money have traditionally ranked high among the most common and serious stressors of family life.

So, what's a responsible grandparent to do? First and foremost, make sure your financial house is in order. There are countless books and online resources to guide you, but I strongly recommend that you engage a licensed financial professional (unless you yourself are one) to figure out what works best in your circumstances.

It must be said that you can't do this at your own peril. There are no hard and fast rules or formulas; it's what works for you and your family.

Dos and Don'ts to Consider

- DO remember that the primary underlying purpose of this initiative from the grandparents' perspective is creating the structure for the siblings and cousins to stay connected and to know on a deeper level what is going on in each other's lives, from the teen years into adulthood. With that in mind, any grandchild, no matter their own immediate family's financial wealth or situation, should feel comfortable to apply.

- DO set a good example by being communicative and candid about financial matters, paving the way for your adult children to do the same. You needn't eschew privacy altogether, but there shouldn't be taboos about discussing important money matters within the family. (Reading and discussing articles about money, for example, is an excellent agenda item for Family Meetings.)

- DO educate yourself about giving wisely. For example, there are estate-planning benefits to making annual monetary gifts directly to grandchildren if you are financially able to do so. At the same time, many people are unaware that a well-meaning contribution to a grandchild's college fund could end up hurting his or her chances of getting financial aid. Once again, it is important to check in with a financial advisor.

- DO make sure that the language in your final directives and your will is explicit and clear. Vague instructions or "surprises" can set the stage for conflict. Because the laws do change and frequently vary from state to state regarding estates, taxation, and healthcare, an attorney who specializes in eldercare is considered the most reliable last word in these matters.

- DON'T put the needs of others before your own financial security. It is tempting to want to lavish gifts upon grandchildren, or to help them (or their parents) out of tight spots. But it is important to make a careful assessment of your own long-term needs first before giving major gifts or even loans to family members. The last thing you want to happen is needing to rely on them later because you've exhausted your resources.

- DON'T "enable" grandchildren by automatically underwriting big-ticket items. Allow them to develop the skills to achieve financial independence. It's bad news all around if their response to your generosity shifts from appreciation to expectation.

My Legacy

What do I dream of when I contemplate *my* legacy? As long as I am around, I want to help my grandchildren pursue their dreams. And it gives me great joy to see them involved in each other's lives, no matter how old they are or where they are in the world.

I dream that the activities the Living Legacy Foundation underwrites will continue to enrich the lives of my family members and the lives of others. I dream that, in the future, my grandchildren will have the means and the motivation to fund the Foundation themselves. I dream that they will build in a philanthropic component and actively support causes they agree are important to all of them. And I dream that they will pass along the Foundation as a treasured family tradition to their grandchildren someday.

Well, I can't see that far into the future. And besides—as my son often reminds me—it's important to savor the present. And I do. I savor the laughter and connection of my grandchildren, those far-flung siblings and cousins, as I watch them discover their individual passions and share their experiences and ideas with each other.

And when they remember dear old Grandma and Grandpa and see in themselves some of us, that is the icing on the cake.

Your Turn: Journaling Expeditions

1. Ask your grandchildren to write you a letter telling you about their dreams for the future.

2. How can you implement the Living Legacy Foundation for your family? Make a draft of potential rules, set a budget, and share it with your adult children to start the ball rolling.

3. What are other ways that you can encourage your grandchildren to connect and engage more deeply with each other? Write down three ideas.

4. Imagine you just won $1,000. Write about how you would divvy it up if you had four jars: Helping, Spending, Saving, and Investing. Explain your reasoning behind your decisions.

CHAPTER 10

A Final Note from the Authors

At the time of this writing, I have moved to live with my adult daughter Ellen and her husband, Don, in Los Angeles. I was so delighted when my granddaughter Kathryn and her then-boyfriend Lance moved to Chicago. We shared wonderful walks together in the Chicago Botanic Garden before she and Lance married and moved to Las Vegas. Less than a year after I moved to LA, she and Lance found a home and relocated again to be near us. Both her parents and I are relishing being so close.

My grandson Ethan visited recently and surprised us by taking a job interview at a nearby synagogue. He has been called back for a second interview and we are hopeful. I could not be more thrilled to see family coming together. Who knows what will be in the future? Maybe we will all end up in Wisconsin. My son Michael is still advocating for the Witkovsky Family Compound—farmland near Madison where each family member could build their own home.

In the meantime, our practice of connecting stays strong. Rabbi Ethan shares his weekly sermons with the whole family by email in advance. We all can watch him deliver it in real time via livestream (along with 100,000 others who tune in from around the globe). I share whatever I write with my family, by email, to inspire conversation. Over the past year I've been writing about #MeToo and hate crimes and all kinds of social issues. The whole family chimes in from coast to coast. My granddaughter Merete shares her papers from college. My grandson Benny promises to send his doctoral thesis as soon as it is done.

What's beautiful about the approaches we've shared in this book is that they grow with you. My son Michael is now a grandfather himself. How wonderful to have something so special in common with my son. That means I'm a great-grandfather. That's a whole new world for my grandchildren when they become parents. Their world is their world. The tools let you enter it, appreciate it, and support it at whatever stage of life your grandchildren are.

On our end, Deanna and I will continue to create new ideas and opportunities for grandparents to be the best that they can be.

It takes constant commitment and effort to develop trust and honesty and to deepen the connectedness between you and your grandchildren and your whole family, at any stage of life. Care for each other. See each other. Love each other. Enter each other's world and see it through their eyes. Keep the creativity, passion, and commitment to your family flowing. The practices you've learned in this book become a way of life. And that is a legacy that will carry on for generations to come.

We leave you with one final journaling expedition:

Ask your grandchildren to write you a letter telling you what they have learned from you.

INDEX OF CONTRIBUTORS

BIBLIOGRAPHY

American Academy of Pediatrics, *Helping Your Child Cope with Life*, Itasca, IL: American Academy of Pediatrics, 2006.

Coleman, Joshua. "Growing Pains." *Greater Good Magazine* (blog). July 8, 2010. https://greatergood. berkeley.edu/article/item/growing_pains.

"Generational Differences Chart." West Midland Family Center. Last updated 2017. http://wmfc.org/uploads/ GenerationalDifferencesChart.pdf/.

Moretti, Marlene M., and Maya Peled. "Adolescent-Parent Attachment: Bonds that Support Healthy Development." *Pediatrics Child Health* 9, no. 8 (2004): 551–555. doi: 10.1093/pch/9.8.551.

Nelson-Kakulla, Brittne. "2018 Grandparents Today National Survey." AARP, 2019. https://www.aarp.org/ content/dam/aarp/research/surveys_statistics/life-leisure/2019/aarp-grandparenting-study.doi.10.26419-2Fres.00289.001.pdf.

Orbuch, Sonia Shainwald. *Here, There Are No Sarahs.* Columbus, OH: Gatekeepers Press, 2009.

"The New American Family: The MetLife Study of Family Structure and Financial Well-Being." MetLife, September 2012. https://www.soa.org/globalassets/assets/Files/Research/Projects/research-2012-metlife-family.pdf.

"The Silent Generation Revisited." *TIME*, June 29, 1970. http://content.time.com/time/subscriber/article/0,33009,878847,00.html.

Vissell, Joyce and Barry. "A Powerful Forgiveness Technique." The Shared Heart Foundation, July 2000. https://sharedheart.org/a-powerful-forgiveness-technique/.

LIST OF PREVIOUS PUBLICATIONS

Witkovsky, Jerry. "Grandchildren: Places and Spaces to Inspire Sharing Stories." *Grand Magazine*, May 23, 2019. https://www.grandmagazine.com/2019/05/grandchildren-places-and-spaces-to-inspire-sharing-stories/.

Witkovsky, Jerry. *The Grandest Love: Inspiring the Grandparent-Grandchild Connection*. Bloomington, IN: Xlibris, 2013.

ABOUT THE AUTHORS

Jerry Witkovsky (MSW, University of Illinois) is a beloved mentor to thousands of individuals and generations of families, thanks to forty-seven years of professional leadership, eighteen of them as General Director of the Jewish Community Centers of Chicago. In 1995 he was named one of the city's "Most Effective Non-Profit CEOs" by *Crain's Chicago Business.*. Since his 1997 retirement, Jerry has focused his considerable energies on grandparenting facilitation—helping multigenerational families work (and play) together to create a rich family life. He has partnered with JCC and YMCA to create a writing prompt program serving over four hundred grandparents on three continents.

He currently spearheads a growing number of school-based programs designed to strengthen connections between grandparents and their teenagers. Learn more at grandparentsunleashed.com.

Deanna Shoss (MA, DePaul University) is a marketer, writer, and interculturalist based in Chicago. As Founder and CEO of Intercultural Talk, Inc., Deanna works with non-digital natives to help them promote their mission-driven businesses or life projects with digital, intercultural, and real-life marketing. She takes an intergenerational approach that combines online communication platforms such as websites/blogs, social media, and video with tried and true practices such as partnership building, email marketing, and in-person events. Previously, Deanna enjoyed eleven years in city government (she personally got the dinosaur at O'Hare International Airport through security), being past President of the League of Chicago Theatres (where she was recognized in 2005 among "Who's Who in Chicago Business" by *Crain's Chicago Business*), leading Public

Relations for McDonald's Owner/Operators of Eastern New England, and directing marketing for Jewish Child & Family Services and JVS Chicago. Deanna writes for the National Diversity Council and is the Tech Columnist for *Grand Magazine*. She speaks Portuguese, Spanish, and French, and is a certified group fitness instructor. Learn more at interculturaltalk.com.